Steph!
Happy! Happy!
Birthday!!
Love you!
Gail

We love being
with you for the
celebrations of your 24th.
What an evening!
Happy Birthday
Love

Happy Birthday---
An evening to remember!
♡ Michele

HAPPY BIRTHDAY
from all at
Jabu Dabi Restaurant!
Cheers.

5-12-12

Stephanie,
    Well girl—you
are always in the
honey pot—and its
not an accident.
You give your
heart & energy to
make us all better.
We love you— Stacy

STEPH!
HAPPY HAPPY DAY!
MMMMMMH.

All Best & Happy
Birthday
[signature]

TIFFANY DIAMONDS

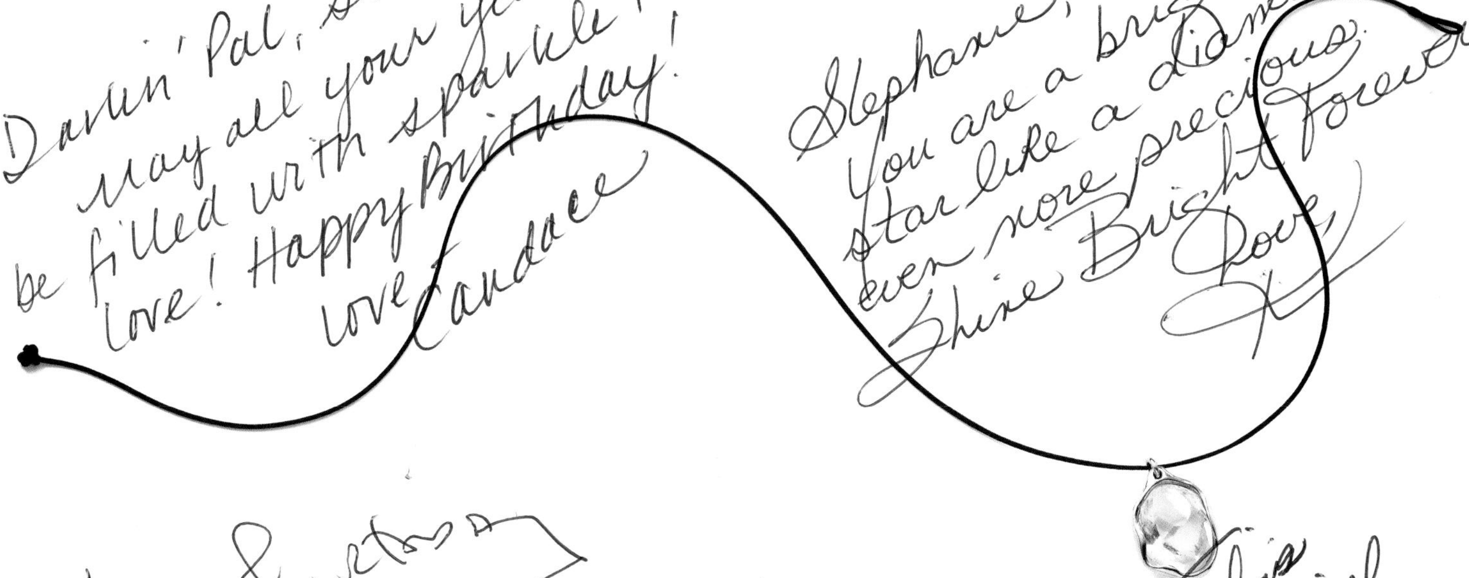

Darlin' Pal, Steph —
May all your years
be filled with sparkle &
love! Happy Birthday!
Love Candace

Stephanie,
You are a bright shining
star like a diamond but
even more precious!
Shine Bright Forever!
Love
[signature]

Happy Birthday
Stephanie!
So happy to your
So tonight.
Emmy

Stephani — This
is a birthday you will
never forget. So great to
have all your friends here.
The Humphrey's house was
incredible! I love
you Bobby

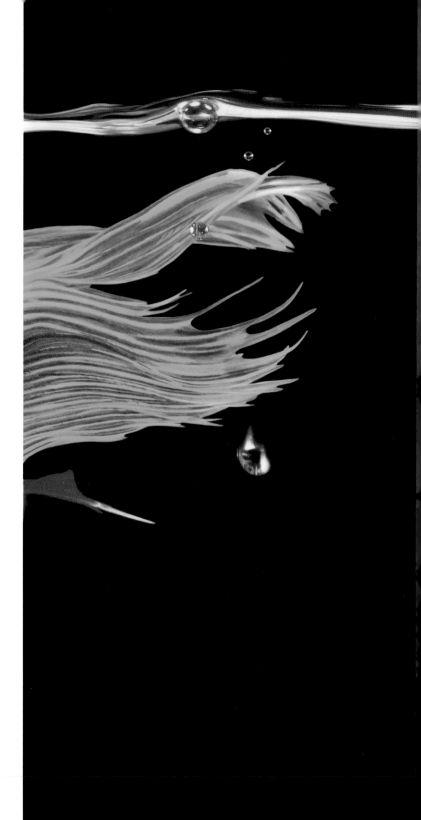

TIFFANY
DIAMONDS

JOHN LORING

ABRAMS, NEW YORK

Hiro

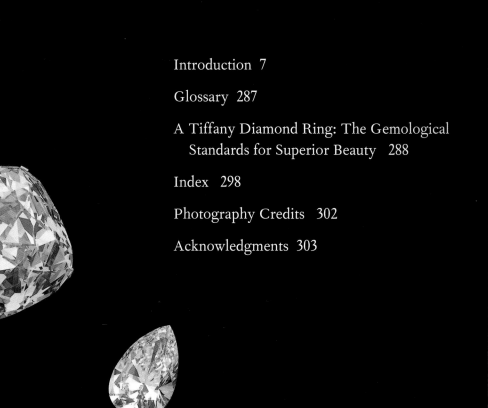

CONTENTS

INTRODUCTION

The greatest value, not merely among precious stones, but among all mankind's possessions, is given to the adamas [diamond], for long known only to kings—and only to a very few of these.

—Pliny, *Historia Naturalis*, AD 77

The intrigue of diamonds, acquired through their association with royalty, and—in the most celebrated cases—with spectacular adventure, did not pass unnoticed in mid-nineteenth-century America, despite the United States' solid, democratic vision of royalty as superfluous. If royals and nobles were eminently dispensable in the minds of good patriotic Americans, their diamonds were as eminently desirable.

There were few diamonds in North America when Charles Lewis Tiffany and John B. Young founded Tiffany & Young at 259 Broadway, New York, in September 1837. However, two and a half years later, when details reached New York of twenty-one-year-old Queen Victoria's wedding to Prince Albert of Saxe-Coburg-Gotha, young women across America doubtlessly dreamed about wearing jewels like the queen's elaborate "Turkish-style" diamond necklace and earrings. At that time neither Tiffany & Co. nor any other American jeweler offered anything approaching the opulence of Victoria's wedding jewels; it would be over eight years before Tiffany's would.

In February 1848 the government of King Louis Philippe and Queen Marie-Amélie of France crumbled. The king abdicated on February 24, and in the ensuing chaos, the aristocracy panicked, remembering all too vividly the bloody events of the 1789 French Revolution. Their diamonds were put on sale for

PAGES 1–3
Elsa Peretti's Diamond in the Rough pendant and diamond-pave Teardrop pendant. Original designs © Elsa Peretti.

OPPOSITE
Lady Astor wearing her tiara topped by the Sancy Diamond to the opening of Parliament on October 27, 1948. In 1906 Nancy Langhorne Shaw (1879–1964), born in the Blue Ridge Mountains of Virginia, married Waldorf Astor, a principal heir to the great Astor fortune; the Sancy was a wedding present from Astor's father. Lady Astor, internationally famous for her beauty and high spirits, represented Plymouth's Sutton Division in the House of Commons from 1919 until 1945.

LEFT
The 55.23-carat pear-shaped Sancy Diamond, once described as "the sphinx of diamonds." Ever since it arrived in France in the late 1500s, the Sancy has had one of the most confusing yet intriguing histories of any of the world's great diamonds. It is now on permanent display at the Louvre (see pages 17–18).

The 44.52-carat Hope Diamond, cut from Louis XIV's Blue Diamond of the Crown (also known as the French Blue and the Tavernier Blue), is one of the most storied diamonds in history (see pages 18, 21–22). Since 1958 it has been in the Smithsonian Institution's Museum of Natural History.

OPPOSITE
Evalyn Walsh McLean (1887–1947) wearing the Hope Diamond as a pendant and a whopping array of other jewelry. Mrs. McLean, heiress to a Colorado gold-mining fortune, was most famous for her ownership of the Hope Diamond, which was rumored to be jinxed. Although she endured an unpleasant divorce and the untimely deaths of two of her four children, she gained a reputation as Washington D.C.'s leading philanthropist and hostess.

whatever price they could fetch, in order to raise money for fleeing the new French Revolution. Good fortune placed Charles Lewis Tiffany's partner, John B. Young, and his jewelry buyer, Thomas Crane Banks, in the middle of Paris on that fateful Thursday, and the pair invested all of the firm's available funds in diamonds and other gemstones.

Back in New York, the windfall spoils of the victorious buying trip were offered by Tiffany's new store, at 271 Broadway. New York had never before seen such a splendid collection of gemstones. On December 13, 1848, the *New York Daily Tribune* ran the following Tiffany ad on page 3:

DIAMONDS ETC.

The undersigned invites all who will have occasion to buy Diamond Jewelry for the holidays to inspect their present stock. It is so usual to claim peculiar facilities and profess an ability of selling at lower prices than others, that the simple assertion to this effect is considered a matter of course and leaves no impression. Feeling that our extraordinary opportunities of buying in quantities, for cash, during the late Revolutions [Hungary and several German states also experienced revolutions in 1848], and subsequent depressions in the European markets, enables us, with entire propriety, to assert the great superiority of our stock of diamonds and other rich jewelry, over any collection ever seen in this country, and our ability to sell at lower prices—and that we are fairly entitled to any benefit that may arise from the matter of fact, we desire to make the assertion so distinctly and formally as to induce all interested to make the necessary inspection and comparison. We beg to observe that the prices to which we invite attention are all marked in plain figures, from which we pledge ourselves not to make the slightest deductions, on any consideration whatever; perfectly confident that the richness and extent of our variety—the beauty and tastefulness of our styles—the freshness of our entire stock, and our low prices, cannot fail to be appreciated by most buyers and will secure us against any competition from old stocks, bought at old prices, that have accumulated here or may be sent out from Europe.

While the ad was entirely accurate, exaggeration played no small role in nineteenth-century marketing. Without the company ever putting it in print, Tiffany's agents leaked the information that Young and Banks had in fact managed to purchase jewels belonging to the French crown, and supposedly among these was the jewel at the center of the Affair of the Diamond Necklace, which had brought disaster down on Marie Antoinette. The necklace, unbeknownst to New Yorkers, was probably never even made; Marie Antoinette had rejected the rock crystal mock-up shown to her by court jewelers Böhmer and Bassange—who had not designed it for her but for King Louis XV's mistress, Mme du Barry. As for the deposed Queen Marie-Amélie, she had never touched the French crown jewels, remembering the 1793 fate of her aunt Marie Antoinette; the personal jewelry Marie-Amélie did wear was all accounted for and in her possession when she fled Paris and its hostile mobs. However, the much-glamorized story of the crown jewels circulated in New York and merited Charles Lewis Tiffany the sobriquet King of Diamonds.

Tiffany's brilliant marketing ploy was so successful that the store not only sold out the 1848 collection of diamonds in short order but also gained near-mythic status. Even a century and a half later one of the world's great auction houses published the apocryphal story in its biography of the jewelry house.

TIFFANY & CO.

By 1848, with the acquisition of the famous diamond girdle once belonging to Marie Antoinette, and twenty-four lots from the French crown jewels, the firm established itself as a significant presence in the American jewelry market. (Sotheby's, Sale 7235, *Important Jewels*. December 9 and 10, 1998, p. 265)

Nearly forty years after the February Revolution of 1848, Tiffany's would, in reality, buy twenty-four lots of magnificent royal jewelry at the May 1887 French Ministry of Finance's Paris auction of "Diamonds of the Crown." But in the meantime, the crown jewels of France would safely spend seventeen years gracing the beautiful Empress Eugénie, wife of Emperor Napóleon III. Only a handful of the jewels purchased had ever been worn by Marie Antoinette. (The majority of her jewels had long before been stolen, during the Revolution in the predawn hours of September 17, 1792, from France's royal furniture repository.)

How well that genius of marketing, Charles Lewis Tiffany, understood that there was truly no one who wouldn't be fascinated by the lore of diamonds, their titled owners, and the adventures surrounding them.

Pliny's precious "adamas" were small diamonds that found their way to the ancient Mediterranean world from Golconda, the fortress city at the center

of diamond trading, located in the state of Hyderabad—the source of Indian diamonds. The Dravidians had mined diamonds since ancient times, yet there is no record of a diamond of any importance before the second millennium A.D. It was a latecomer to the world of gems, but once it arrived, the diamond moved to first place. No other stone has excited such extraordinary excesses and intrigues.

Until 1725, when diamonds were discovered in northeastern Brazil, all diamonds came from India via Golconda (with the exception of a small production from Borneo), and the majority of history's fabled diamonds are "Golcondas": the Koh-i-noor, the Regent, the Sancy, the Hope, etc.

Their histories are remarkable and are worth retelling: The Koh-i-noor, according to tradition, was found in the Godavari River thousands of years ago and worn by a mythic hero of that great Hindu epic, *Mahabharata*. In reality it was the property of the Rajas of Malwa for generations (but not for millennia) until taken by a neighboring prince in the early 1300s.

In 1526, with the Muslim conquest of India, the 186-carat stone became the property of the Mogul emperors, and it remained so (in the treasury of Delhi) until the Persians, led by Nadir Shah, conquered Delhi in 1739. Nadir Shah named the stone *Koh-i-noor*, or *mountain of light*, and took it to Persia, where it inspired a grisly and intricate series of assassinations, until it was taken by Ranjit Singh, the "Lion of the Punjab," who wore it in an armlet. After Ranjit's death, the diamond was sent to the Punjab treasury at Lahore, where it remained until Lahore was taken over by the British in 1849, at which point it became the property of Queen Victoria. The old Indian cutting did not suit the thirty-year-old queen, so she had it recut in Amsterdam at the Coster factory (then the largest diamond-cutting factory in the world) at a reported cost of $40,000. The newly cut and more brilliant stone of 105.60 carats was set into a circlet to be worn in the queen's hair. (The merit of that procedure, which took away much of the stone's patina, is disputable; but even reduced to just over 105 carats, the Koh-i-noor was at the time the largest diamond in England's crown jewels.) Today it remains at the front of the crown made in 1937 for the late Queen Mother Elizabeth, set in the cross pattee.

Queen Victoria's Koh-i-noor had a worthy rival in the 143-carat Regent Diamond (in the crown jewels of France from 1717). Discovered in 1701 in the mines at Partial, about 150 miles southwest of Golconda, the stone originally weighed 410 carats. The enslaved miner who found the stone decided to steal it. He cut his leg and hid the diamond in the blood-soaked bandages; then he made his way to the seacoast, where he struck up a deal with an unsavory English sea captain, who gave him passage "to a distant land" in exchange for half interest in

The royal family on the balcony of Buckingham Palace after the coronation of King George VI on May 12, 1937. At left his consort, Queen Elizabeth (1900–2002) wears the crown shown on page 14. The front of the king's crown is set with the 317.40-carat Second Star of Africa, also known as Cullinan II. His mother, Queen Mary, wears the 94.40-carat Cullinan III and the 63.60-carat Cullinan IV as pendants. (The Cullinans were cut from a 3,106-carat rough diamond found in 1905; the largest, the 530.20-carat Great Star of Africa, is in the royal scepter.) Princess Elizabeth (now Queen Elizabeth II) and Princess Margaret wear gold coronets.

Crown made by Garrard & Co. for the 1937 coronation of King George VI's consort, Queen Elizabeth. The cross pattee at the front is set with the 105.60-carat Koh-i-noor Diamond, the most famous diamond in history (see page 13). Queen Victoria believed the superstition that India would be lost to the British Empire if the Koh-i-noor were worn by a king, so she bequeathed it to her daughter-in-law Alexandra, Princess of Wales, and entailed it to the consorts of future kings. Queen Alexandra (consort of Edward VII) wore it in her crown for her 1902 coronation, as did Queen Mary (consort of George V) for her 1911 coronation.

the priceless diamond. The captain took the stone and gave the miner passage "to a distant land" by tossing him overboard, where he was dispatched by the local harbor sharks. The captain (who soon after committed suicide) obtained about $5,000 for his diamond from a Parsi merchant, who in turn sold it to Sir Thomas Pitt, the English governor of Fort St. George in Madras, for twenty times what he had paid.

Back in London, Pitt had the massive rough diamond cut down to a 143-carat cushion-shaped brilliant and, after many unsuccessful attempts to rebuild the Pitt fortunes with his unique stone, sold it for about 2 million francs to the Duke of Orléans, who ruled France during the minority of his nephew, King Louis XV. Five years later the king came of age and had the court jeweler, Claude Rondé, set the Regent in his coronation crown. (He had worn it only once before, on March 21, 1721—set in a bow of pearls and other diamonds—on the shoulder of his cloak, while receiving Turkish ambassadors.)

The Regent was frequently worn by Louis XV's wife, Queen Marie Leszczynska, in her hair or as a necklace pendant. It remained in the crown jewels of France until it was stolen during the great jewel robbery of September 17, 1792. Fortunately, the thieves, unsure of what to do with some of the world's greatest diamonds, put them in makeshift hiding places, so the Regent was soon recovered where it had been stashed—in the rafters of a Paris attic.

Napoléon I had the Regent mounted in the hilt of his sword, but following the restoration of the Bourbon monarchy, the Regent apparently was not worn by the King Louis XVIII. Charles X briefly had it set in the fleur-de-lis of his crown. It was not worn by Louis Philippe or Marie-Amélie. (Both, as previously stated, refused to wear any of the crown jewels.)

After having been dazzled at a Windsor Castle reception by the newly recut Koh-i-noor perched in the hair of hostess Queen Victoria, the twenty-five-year-old Empress Eugénie of France had the Regent set in a coronet for the opening of the Paris Exposition of 1855, where it was later exhibited.

The Regent remained in Paris after the fall of Napoléon III and the Second Empire in 1870. The Republican government exhibited it at the Paris Exposition of 1878 (discouraging Charles Lewis Tiffany from exhibiting the newly cut and somewhat smaller 128.54-carat Tiffany Diamond).

Given the opportunity, Tiffany would most likely have bought the Regent in 1887; however, the Ministry of Finance did not include it in the auction of the French crown jewels (where Tiffany was the largest buyer) but retained it as part of the national patrimony of France. Today it rests on public display in the Apollo Gallery of the Louvre.

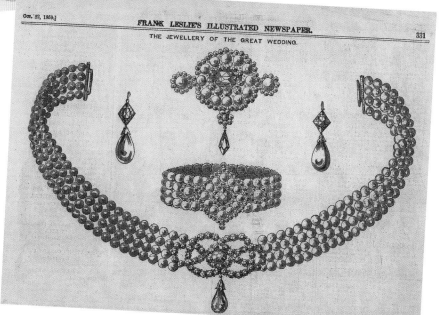

FRANK LESLIE'S ILLUSTRATED NEWSPAPER.

THE JEWELLERY OF THE GREAT WEDDING.

331

On October 13, 1859, a rich Cuban sugar planter, Don Estéban Santa Cruz de Oviedo, married Frances Amelia Bartlett in New York (see pages 52, 58, 60, 63). Undoubtedly at Charles Lewis Tiffany's instigation, the press covered their "Diamond Wedding" extensively, but cynics noted that the groom was about six inches shorter and forty years older than the bride. Above: The groom with his bride and her bridesmaids at the wedding in old Saint Patrick's Cathedral on Mott Street. Below: Tiffany's pearl-and-diamond parure for the Oviedo-Bartlett wedding.

GRAND BALL GIVEN BY THE CITIZENS OF NEW YORK AT THE ACADEMY OF MUSIC, IN HONOR OF THE PRINCE OF WALES—THE PRINCE OPENING THE BALL.—SEE PAGE 836.

The Sancy, a much smaller (55.23-carat) stone from the French crown jewels, has effected the greatest adventures of any of its peers, although—as with many famed diamonds—untangling myth and actual history is virtually impossible.

According to legend, an Indian trader appeared in Constantinople around 1570 with a large and—for the time—beautifully faceted diamond. He eventually found a buyer in Seigneur Nicolas Harlay de Sancy (1546–1629), the master of requests to the French Parliament. On the death of King Charles IX, his younger brother, the sybaritic and depraved Henry III, ascended the French throne. His scandal-ridden reign, masterminded by his mother, Catherine de Médicis, would last for fifteen years. Henry appointed Sancy ambassador to Switzerland in 1575, and in return Sancy wisely loaned his prized diamond to the luxury-addicted king, who used it to ornament the caps he wore, indoors and out.

When the hated Henry III was assassinated in 1589, the 261-year-old Valois dynasty ended, and Henry de Bourbon, King of Navarre, was named successor. Henry IV's claim to the throne only succeeded through the help of Sancy, who was then colonel general of an army of 12,000 Swiss mercenaries, bought with monies raised by pawning his adventure-loving diamond. Upon Henry of Navarre's crowning as Henry IV of France, Sancy was named superintendent of finance by his grateful king and quickly redeemed the already well-traveled stone.

France was bankrupt, however, so Sancy sent the diamond off with a servant in search of a new loan to float his own finances or the national economy. News of the diamond was leaked, and thieves attacked the servant who immediately, and apparently invisibly, managed to swallow the diamond. The thwarted adventurers, not finding the stone, murdered the poor man, whose body was recovered and opened some days later by Sancy, who found the diamond. It was still for sale at an asking price of 140,000 ecus.

The king wanted to buy the diamond for himself at half price, but it was doubtful he could pay even the 70,000 ecus, so Sancy resolved the problem in 1605 by selling his diamond to the more financially stable James I of England for the lesser sum of 60,000 ecus, payable in three cash installments.

The diamond passed from King James I to his extravagant son, Charles I, who married Henrietta Maria of France, Henry IV's daughter. Charles I was in grave financial trouble and plagued by the Puritan revolution. In 1645 he had Queen Henrietta Maria slip off to Holland with the Sancy, where she sold it along with another large diamond, the Mirror of Portugal, to the Duke of Épernon—in exchange for settling 427,566 livres of Charles I's debts. Épernon then sold the stones to Cardinal Mazarin, since 1642 the first minister of France and a great collector of diamonds. When he died in 1661, Mazarin left his diamonds to Louis XIV. Like the Regent, the Sancy later ornamented the crown of Louis XV and was a favorite bauble of both Marie Leszczynska and Marie Antoinette. It too disappeared in the crown jewel robbery of 1792.

About five years later, the Sancy resurfaced in Madrid, pawned for 1 million francs to the Marquis of Iranda, from whom it passed on to Prime Minister Godoy of Spain. In Paris, Godoy sold the Sancy in 1828 to Count Nicholas Demidoff, who died later the same year. Demidoff's son Anatole probably inherited the diamond at that point, at the age of fifteen. Anatole later married Napoléon III's cousin, Princess Mathilde Bonaparte, and she may well have put the Sancy Diamond up for sale via court jeweler Bapst in 1867, as she saw the Second Empire under her cousin beginning to falter. In any case, the Sancy reappeared at the Paris Exposition of 1867, exhibited by Bapst, who offered it for 1 million francs.

Nineteen years after the fall of the Second Empire, at the time of the Paris Exposition of 1889, the Sancy Diamond was owned and exhibited by Lucien Falize, a leading Paris jeweler (who, incidentally, made jewelry for Tiffany & Co.). In 1892 the diamond was sold to William Waldorf Astor, grandson of John Jacob Astor (reputedly the richest man in the United States at that time). Astor had served in the New York Legislature and was the U.S. minister to Italy from 1881 to 1885. (In 1899 he became a British citizen; he was made a viscount in 1917.) In 1906 Astor gave the Sancy to his politically active daughter-in-law, the former Nancy Langhorne of Virginia, who in 1919 became the first woman to take her seat in the House of Commons. On state occasions Nancy Astor wore the Sancy in her tiara (see illustration, page 6).

Finally, in 1978, Viscount William Waldorf Astor IV sold the Sancy to the Bank of France and the Museums of France for $1 million. Today it is displayed alongside the Regent Diamond in the Apollo Gallery of the Louvre.

The Hope Diamond, the most important blue diamond ever discovered, is one of the two most celebrated stones now in the United States (along with the Tiffany Diamond). It has invited as much speculation as any of its equally famous Golconda cousins, if not more.

Now weighing in at 44 carats, the Hope was a much larger stone (around 110.5 carats) when it was discovered in the Kollur mine, near Golconda, in the mid-seventeenth century (ca. 1642). The great adventurer, traveling merchant, and chronicler of diamonds Jean Baptiste Tavernier brought the blue diamond back from India in 1669 and sold it to Louis XIV (who was Tavernier's customer for 44 of the finest large diamonds and 1,122 smaller stones—for a total price

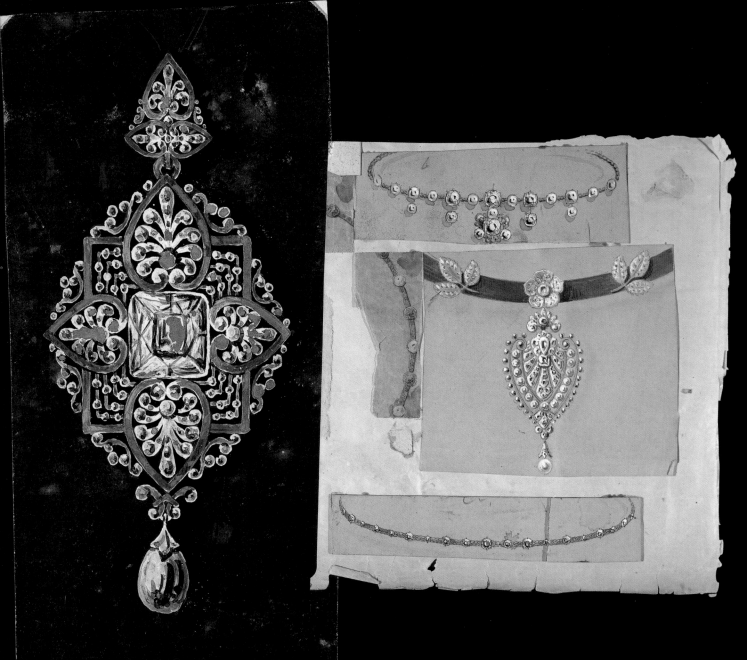

of 897,731 livres). The Tavernier Blue or French Blue was recut by Louis XIV's court jeweler, Pitau, in 1673 into a heart-shaped stone of 69.03 carats, which the Sun King wore as a pendant on a ribbon around his neck.

Louis XIV's great-grandson, Louis XV, had his court jeweler, Jacquemin, mount the then-called Blue Diamond of the Crown in a decoration of the Order of the Golden Fleece which he too wore on a ribbon around his neck, as Louis XVI did after him. (Marie Antoinette certainly never wore this exclusively male ornament of an order to which she did not belong.)

During the French Revolution, the Blue Diamond of the Crown, then valued at 3 million francs, was stored in the Garde-Meuble. It was stolen during the notorious robbery of September 17, 1792. Unlike the Regent and the Sancy, the Hope did not resurface for twenty years.

Then, in September 1812, a 44-carat brilliant-cut, deep blue diamond belonging to dealer Daniel Eliason popped up in London. The stone was purchased between 1824 and 1830 by a wealthy banker and important collector of gems, Henry Philip Hope. When the Hope collection was catalogued by gem expert Bram Hertz in 1839, the "Hope" diamond appeared at the top of the list.

Henry Philip Hope's nephew Henry Thomas Hope later bought the great blue diamond from his uncle's estate and displayed it at the London Crystal Palace Exhibition of 1851, as well as at the Paris Exposition of 1855. The Hope Diamond was then inherited by Hope's widow, who in 1887 left it to her grandson Lord Henry Francis Hope Pelham-Clinton-Hope (younger brother of the Duke of Newcastle). In 1894 Lord Henry married American actress May Yohé. The following year he went bankrupt, but he managed to hold on to his diamond until 1901.

On November 13, 1901, the Hope Diamond was finally sold out of the Hope family to Adolf Weil of 25 Hatton Gardens, London—who was probably buying for Simon Frankel of Joseph Frankel's and Sons of New York—for the sum of £33,000. It then passed into the hands of the Turkish sultan Abd al-Hamid II, who owned it until he was deposed in 1909.

When the sultan's jewels were put on sale on June 24, 1909, the Hope was bought by a Paris dealer named Rosenau. Two years later, the famous Paris jeweler Pierre Cartier brought the stone to New York and sold it to gold-mining heiress Evalyn Walsh McLean, of Washington, D.C. Mrs. McLean wore the Hope Diamond suspended from a diamond necklace until her death on April 26, 1947.

Finally, in April 1949, the New York diamond dealer Harry Winston bought most of Mrs. McLean's jewels, and on November 10, 1958, he presented the Hope to the Smithsonian Institution for its Hall of Gems, where it resides today.

The Hope was undoubtedly cut from Tavernier's and Louis XIV's Blue Diamond of the Crown, as up until the 1912 appearance of the Hope in London, the only other deep blue diamond of any great size to have been found was the blue diamond belonging to the kings of Bavaria, the "Wittelsbach," and it was accounted for. The Wittelsbach began its European career as a 35.32-carat rough diamond given by Philip IV of Spain to his daughter, the Infanta Margareta Teresa, as a wedding present when she married the emperor of Austria, Leopold I, in 1664. It then went by descent to the kings of Bavaria, who owned it until 1918, when King Louis III abdicated following World War I (almost one hundred years after the London appearance of the Hope). The Wittelsbach has been in a private collection since 1964.

Of all the stories that surround diamonds, none can equal—or is so elaborate and so purposely confusing as—the Affair of the Diamond Necklace, an incredible and scandalous sequence of intrigues, frauds, lies, betrayals, and politics that contributed to the French Revolution of 1789 and the fall of the French monarchy.

The books and essays on the subject (beginning with file Y2B1417 in the National Archives in Paris, which contains all the papers presented at the French parlement's trial of the conspirators on May 30, 1786) would fill a small library. Only a few truths can be unraveled from nearly two hundred years of writing on the subject, starting with the vitriolic and self-serving memoirs of the chief conspirator, Countess Jeanne de La Motte, which were published in London in 1789, two years after she had escaped from the Paris prison of the Salpêtrière, where she was confined for her villainy.

The affair begins in 1784 with the court jewelers to Louis XVI and Marie Antoinette—Böhmer and Bassange—who hoped to sell a monumental necklace combined with a corsage ornament (called a stomacher or girdle) to the queen, whose love of diamonds was remarkable and inappropriate at a time when financial problems plagued France.

The jewelers made a rock crystal mock-up of their design, a 647-stone whopper that would weigh around 2,850 carats if completed. The mock-up was shown to the queen with a suggested price of 160,000 livres. The queen refused, rightly suggesting that the money would be better spent on a new ship for the French navy. She may not have liked the heavy and clumsy design, having a marked taste for light settings that showed off individual stones, rather than great massings of diamonds in a single piece.

Böhmer and Bassange were in despair at the refusal. They had already purchased a quantity of diamonds for the necklace and overextended their

3

50 Dias

4

45 Dias

5

6

35 Dias

finances, having been misled as to the queen's desires. The jewelers tried to sell their design to other royal houses (including the Portuguese house of Breganza, which, of course, controlled the Brazilian diamond market and could have had the necklace completed with no strain on the Portuguese economy). All refused.

Meanwhile, an important member of France's nobility, Cardinal Prince Louis de Rohan, had fallen out of favor with the king and queen. Rohan was a silly and gullible fop surrounded by charlatans and flatterers, one of whom—an adventuress and court intriguer who claimed to be a descendant of the Valois kings, Countess Jeanne de Saint-Rémy de Valois de Luz de La Motte—rose to the forefront.

Mme de La Motte convinced the credulous Louis de Rohan that the queen

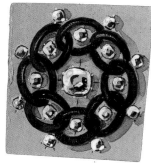

secretly wished to buy Böhmer and Bassange's necklace but lacked sufficient funds for it without asking the king for money, and the king would have no part of purchasing jewels in such difficult times. The countess further convinced the foolish Rohan that his only passport to the queen's favor—as he was a rich man—was to help the queen obtain the necklace.

At the end of February 1785 they concocted a contract, which Rohan signed, to arrange for the purchase of the necklace. The countess took the contract, secretly forged the queen's signature on it, and returned it to Rohan. Böhmer and Bassange, desperate to make the sale, believed the hoax and accepted a down payment. In a charade clumsily but successfully staged by Mme de La Motte, the necklace (or a box containing diamonds selected for it) was taken to Versailles in the dead of night to be "secretly" delivered to the queen. At

The 128.54-carat Tiffany Diamond. Mined in South Africa in 1877 and cut in Paris the following year, it has 41 facets on the crown (including the table) and 41 facets on the pavilion (including the culet). Since 1878 it has been on display at Tiffany & Co.'s New York store, except for special exhibitions. According to George Frederick Kunz: "The Tiffany Company's large yellow diamond . . . is absolutely perfect, is a 'double-deck' cut brilliant, and it is termed, and is undoubtedly, the finest large yellow diamond known. . . . One of the most pleasing features is that it not only retains its rich yellow color by artificial light, but is even more beautiful by day. . . . Because of its deep color, this is a finer stone than the historical Star of the South (125 carats), which was purchased by the Mahratta, ruler of Baroda, for four hundred thousand francs at the French Exposition, 1867. It also rivals the Florentine, which according to Schrauf's determination, weighed 133 3/5 carats, and was sold for two million florins, but it is only a long double rose or drop, not a brilliant." (*Science*, August 5, 1887, vol. 10, no. 235, pp. 69–70).

OPPOSITE
In 1976 Jean Schlumberger designed this jeweled bird perched on a topaz and called it Bird-on-a-Rock. Shown here is a version of Bird-on-a-Rock with the Tiffany Diamond as they were displayed at the 1995–96 Schlumberger exhibition at the Musée des Art Décoratifs in Paris. Schlumberger (1907–1987), the son of an Alsatian textile manufacturer, began designing jewelry for the Paris couturiere Elsa Schiaparelli in 1936. He opened his first New York shop in 1946 and joined Tiffany & Co. in March 1956.

Above: Diamond-and-gold-bow floral corsage ornament with pearl drops, ca. 1880, placed upon an archival drawing for a similar diamond-bow corsage ornament. Below: Two ca. 1875–80 drawings for a diamond brooch centered by a large cushion-cut brown diamond and hung with a "Cape color" (pale yellow) briolette diamond drop. They may be studies for a jewel shown at the Philadelphia Centennial Exposition of 1876 or the Paris Exposition Universelle of 1878.

OPPOSITE
In the center is a ca. 1875–80 design for a crossover bracelet with a 5.81-carat cushion-shaped diamond and a 5.13-carat emerald. The bracelet was priced at $15,000; Tiffany's cost was $10,773.

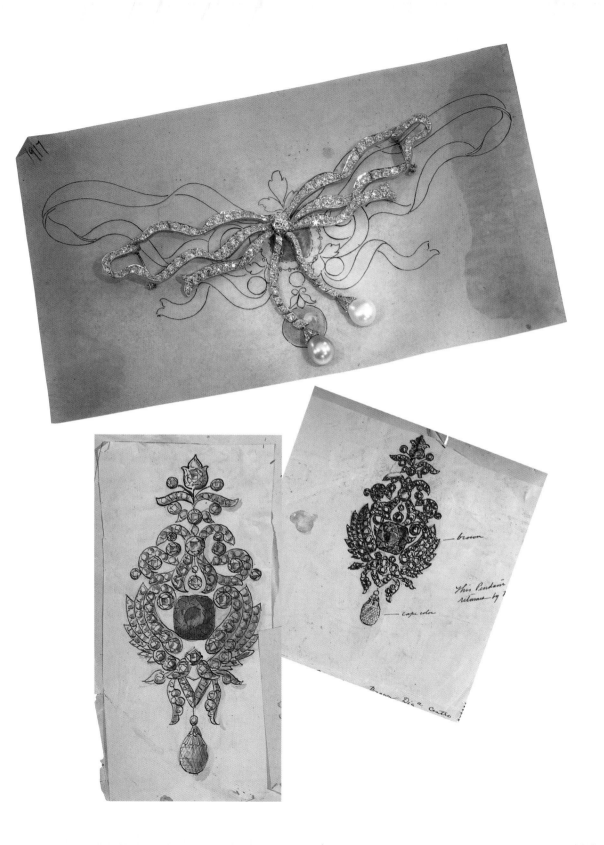

904 30195 + 15.000

1 Emerald ⟨ 5"8 cvsi.

1 Rt „ 5¾4"16 sdsd eosd.

        mtg ∧rd.

          sd∧z1.

4 103

Versailles, La Motte's paramour, Rétaux de Villette, posing as the queen's agent, took possession of the box purportedly containing the necklace. Once the conspirators were dispersed, Villette gave the box to La Motte, who dashed back to Paris with her loot.

In later memoirs (she wrote two versions, one in 1789, the other in 1791), Mme de La Motte claims to have broken up the necklace and sent her husband, Count Marc Antoine Nicholas de La Motte, to London to sell the stones. (There was probably no necklace to break up, only loose stones—and these La Motte did in fact sell in London.)

The hoodwinked jewelers complained of the diamonds' theft by Cardinal de Rohan and Countess de La Motte. The cardinal was arrested on August 15 and the countess on August 18, 1785. Louis XVI referred the Affair of the Diamond Necklace to the Paris parlement on September 19.

An archenemy of the king and queen, the Baron de Breteuil, headed the investigation—which lasted until May 30, 1786, when the case was decided by parlement. The verdicts against the Cardinal de Rohan and the Countess de La Motte were read on May 31.

The Baron de Breteuil made sure that the queen's knowledge of the whole sordid affair was left open to question, and thereby permanently damaged her reputation. He also made sure that when the records of the Affair of the Diamond Necklace were placed in the National Archives in the two large cardboard boxes, they contained neither Rohan's contract (with La Motte's forgeries of Marie Antoinette's handwriting), nor Rohan's handwritten confession of August 15, 1785 (the day of his arrest), nor the queen's seven-page explanation of the events. All vanished without a trace.

The Cardinal de Rohan clearly did not regain Marie Antoinette's favor. In fact, after the affair was judged, she called him "a vile and clumsy counterfeiter" in a letter to her brother, Emperor Joseph of Austria, dated September 19, 1786. And the crown jewelers did not regain their diamonds. In 1785 the Count de La Motte sold twenty-two diamonds to one jeweler (Gray's of Bond Street) and the remaining diamonds to other jewelers. Gray's made the diamonds into a single long-chain necklace of twenty-two stones, weighing a total of 140 carats, and sold it to the Duchess of Sutherland. The stones of another jeweler were made into a necklace that sold for 975 pounds to John Frederick Sackville, third Duke of Dorset, in 1790. (The Duke of Dorset was the British ambassador at Versailles from 1785 to 1789 and must have been amused by this souvenir of the Affair of the Diamond Necklace.)

Both the Sutherland and Sackville diamonds remain in the families' collections to this day. In 1955, both necklaces were on display at the Marie Antoinette Bicentennial Exhibit at Versailles, along with a third necklace of six pear-shaped diamonds purportedly destined for the top and center pendants of the "Queen's Necklace." In addition, the Geneva jeweler Lucien Bessanger loaned the rock crystal mock-up that had been passed down in his family from his great-great-grandfather Paul Bassange—all that remained of the necklace and probably all there ever was, except for a few dozen diamonds stolen from Böhmer and Bassange by Jeanne de La Motte and sold by her husband shortly thereafter.

Needless to say, the prominence of the players; the short-lived success of Mme de La Motte's preposterous plot; the gory executions of the king and queen on January 21, 1793, and October 16, 1793, respectively; the disappearance of the three principal pieces of evidence from the National Archives of France; and the further fabrications of Jeanne de La Motte in her memoirs of 1789 and 1791 all fueled the fires of conjecture. Anyone who could read had probably read one version or another of the famous affair by the time Tiffany purchased diamonds during the comparatively minor French Revolution of 1848 (the February Revolution).

Fresh fuel was added to the fire when a mysterious woman who called herself only "Countess Jeanne" died in Paris in May 1844—inspiring a new round of speculation. (The real Countess de La Motte had died long before on August 23, 1791, reportedly falling from a window in London as she was fleeing creditors.) The legend of the necklace was kept alive by "Countess Jeanne" and other imposters.

In February 1848 it is likely that several of the panic-stricken French nobles selling their diamonds to Tiffany's buyers John B. Young and Thomas Crane Banks confided to the young Americans that their mothers or grandmothers had been close friends of the tragic Queen Marie Antoinette. They probably asserted that only the desperate circumstances of the moment could force them to separate themselves from their treasured stones—preserved from the famous diamond necklace or from a girdle of their late beloved queen—diamonds that had been passed down in their families from sources too noble and too close to power to mention.

In any case, New Yorkers were all too happy to accept the rumors about Tiffany's new diamonds as true, and the 1848 imports sold out. The rumors remain to this day.

And so, in the Affair of the Diamond Necklace, Thomas Carlyle concluded the following in his 151-page essay on the subject (written eleven years before Tiffany's windfall purchases):

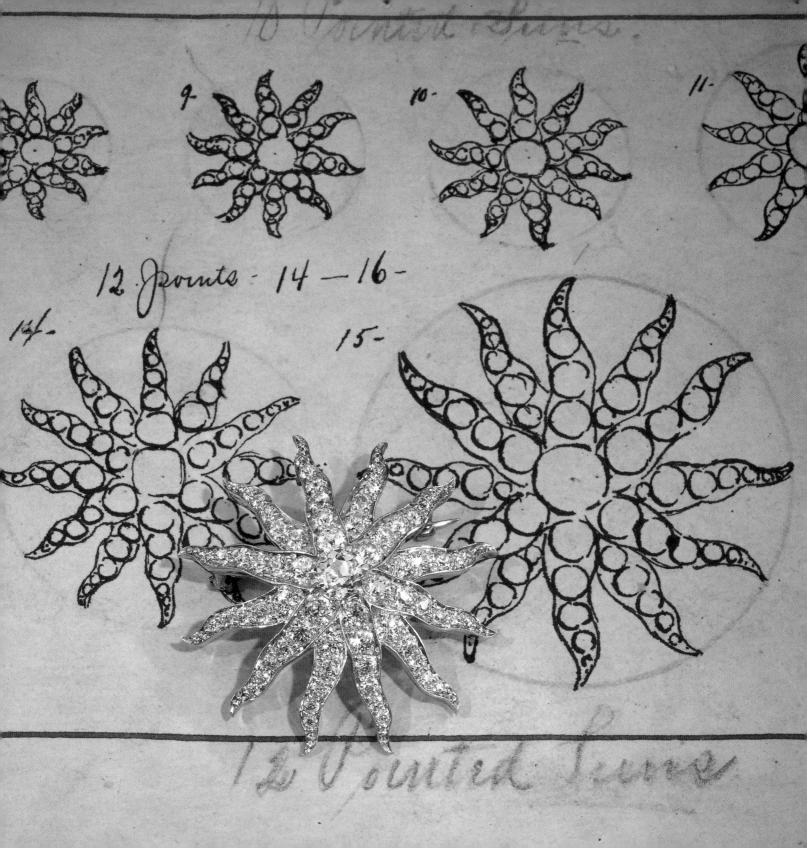

9.

10.

11.

12. Points = 14 — 16 —

14.

15.

Here, then, our little labour ends. The Necklace was, and is no more: the stones of it again "circulate in Commerce," and may give rise to what other histories we know not. The Conquerors of it, every one that trafficked in it, have they not all had their due, which was Death? This little Business, like a little cloud, bodied itself forth in skies clear to the unobservant: but with such hues of deep-tinted villany, dissoluteness, and general delirium as, to the observant, betokened it electric. (Thomas Carlyle, "The Diamond Necklace," *Frazer's Magazine*, London, 1837)

Having fulfilled his goal of marketing diamonds with noble provenance to his status-conscious clientele, Charles Lewis Tiffany continued triumphantly on his way as New York's King of Diamonds.

These ca. 1900 Paulding
Farnham drawings for a
tiara have the fleur-de-lis
motif often used in tiaras.
Farnham was Tiffany &
Co.'s chief jewelry
designer from the mid-
1880s until 1902.

OPPOSITE
Ca. 1880 tiara design
with 9 large (1.51- to
4.61-carat) diamonds
and 287 small diamonds.
Tiffany & Co.'s cost was
27,085 francs, or around
$5,400. The tiara was
probably made at the
Tiffany branch in Paris.

1 Brillts K 4 1/2" 16 @ 5 d 2   f c s d x

2 do „ 6 17/16   0 x 2   x d x d

4 do „ 8 31/16 '32 x d 2   E x x E S

2 do „ 3 1/32   x n x E   S n x E

26 do „ 12 7/8 31/32 n n d   x E x x

3 do „ 2 7/8 11/32   c E d   S x x E

195 do . 13 7/8   x 2 d   x x x x

63 Roses „ 7/16   x E d   s d x

                    mtg & box   s c d x
                                 ───────
                                 x x d o x

The Tiffany Company No. 2 (see Figs. 8, 9) weighs 77 carats, is of a light-yellowish color, is absolutely perfect, and is one of the few large stones that have been cut for beauty and not for weight. It is so evenly cut that it will stand on the culet, which is only of the regular size.

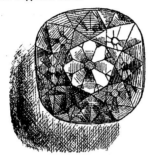

FIGS. 8, 9.   FIGS. 10, 11.

Figs. 10 and 11 show a fine yellow diamond, weighing 51½ carats, also from South Africa, and recently recut by Tiffany & Co. in New York City. It is absolutely perfect, and without flaws. It measures 22 mm. (⅞ of an inch) in length, 22 mm. in width, 23.75 mm. (31/32 of an inch) at the corners, and 15.75 mm. (⅝ of an inch) in thickness; there are 73 facets on the crown or upper side of the stone, and 49 facets on the pavilion or back; and the cutting, which is that of a double-deck brilliant with some of the lower crown-facets divided in two, is quite unique, forming a remarkably beautiful gem.

GEORGE F. KUNZ.

New York, Aug. 1.

ABOVE

This drawing from the *London Illustrated News* on April 23, 1887, shows many of the jewels for sale at the auction of the crown jewels of France held at the Louvre from May 12 to 23, 1887, where Tiffany & Co. was the leading purchaser (see pages 83, 88, 91). Only a few of these pieces were made before the reign of Napoléon III, but many were set with gemstones that had descended through the Bourbon royal family. Most were broken up into multiple lots and sublots to make them more readily marketable to the jewelry trade. The jewels purchased by Tiffany & Co. in this drawing include parts of a diamond comb made by the Paris jewelers Albert and Frédéric Bapst in 1856 for Empress Eugénie; a 176-carat buckle for a girdle made for Empress Eugénie by Bapst in 1868; and a hair ornament from a sapphire parure made by Bapst for the Duchess of Angoulême, daughter of Louis XVI and Marie Antoinette.

BELOW

Lot no. 43 in the French crown jewel auction was listed as "Broche Sévigné"; it had been the centerpiece of the "garland of currant leaves" diamond parure that Bapst made for Empress Eugénie in July 1855. The brooch was set with 321 diamonds weighing a total of 173 carats. The top central 20.03-carat diamond had been purchased by Napoléon I from Étienne Nitot on April 10, 1810, for 78,000 francs. Napoléon's second wife, Empress Marie-Louise, had worn it in a hair ornament (*cache-peigne*) and it was later set in the front of Charles X's crown. Tiffany & Co. paid 120,100 francs (then equivalent to about $18,500) for the brooch and sold it to Cornelia Martin, heiress to a New York logging fortune.

Lot no. 10 at the French crown jewel auction was a *collier aux quatre rivières,* a four-strand diamond necklace, which originally had two large shoulder bows. Set with 222 diamonds weighing a total of 363 carats, it was made by Bapst for Empress Eugénie in 1863–64. On May 12, 1887, Tiffany & Co. paid 183,000 francs for the four-strand necklace (the bows were auctioned separately) and sold the necklace to Joseph Pulitzer, publisher of the New York *World*. Pulitzer's wife, Kate, wore the necklace to a party in Paris the next day.

Tiffany's kingdom was New York, and in 1848 New York was a relatively small city of 500,000 people. Before the Civil War (1861–65), the fortunes of New York's citizens were small (compared to today's standards), and so were their jewels. Diamonds of over 5 carats were considered unsalable in the late 1840s and 1850s, not because New York society considered them ostentatious, but because New Yorkers simply did not have the money to buy them.

Spurred on by the publicity and the windfall profits of his 1848 diamond sale, Tiffany negotiated in 1850 the opening of a branch of his company in Paris at 59, rue de Richelieu. Here his new partner, Gideon F. T. Reed, could procure the latest French jewelry fashions to send to New York and offer more important stones to Parisian customers—who were not at all intimidated by diamonds of over 5 carats.

Tiffany & Co.'s first diamond jewelry register indicates that the firm's trade in diamonds and diamond jewelry began in earnest in early 1853, with the move to the first full-scale Tiffany store at 550 Broadway. Both prices and carat weights continued to be modest by today's standards. A ring stone of slightly over 3.5 carats was registered on May 20, 1853, for $300, which, with Tiffany's standard 33⅓ percent markup on jewelry would have brought the selling price to just $400. Less important diamonds were a fraction of this. The 1853 ledger lists them at 1 carat/$30; ½ carat/$15; ¼ carat/$7; ⅛ carat/$3.75; 1/16 carat/$1.87; 1/32 carat/95¢; 1/64 carat/$47¢. Yellow diamonds appear to have been even less. On August 8, 1853, ring no. 1809, with a 3.31-carat yellow brilliant was registered for $130 ($175 retail). Single-cut melee was registered at $25 per carat.

The ledger confirms Charles Lewis Tiffany's view that diamonds of over 5 carats were a difficult sell. The largest brilliant from the 1850s was a 10.50-carat stone listed on July 21, 1853, as included in a necklace of "7 large and 30 smaller pearls—$4,000." No charge is listed for the 10.50-carat brilliant, indicating that it already belonged to the client. (It was quite possibly bought from Tiffany's 1848 diamond sale and kept unset for the elapsed years.) Another large brilliant of slightly over 8.50 carats is listed on October 5, 1853, as an unset stone, in stock, with the notation "sovereign"—possibly indicating that it, too, came from the 1848 "royal" diamond collection.

Brilliants of between 3.50 and almost 5.0 carats appear quite frequently in the registers of the 1850s, for use in rings, earrings, and "pins"—often stickpins for men. Prices remained modest, as did markup. A pin containing a 5.13-carat stone was registered on November 23, 1855, for a cost of $896.28, plus $12 for the gold stickpin mount, totaling $908.28. It was sold for $1200—just under the traditional 33⅓ percent markup.

OPPOSITE

Left: Diamond buckle made by Bapst for Empress Eugénie in 1868. Tiffany & Co. paid 132,500 francs for the buckle at the auction. Its central 25.82-carat blue-tinged diamond —purchased by Napoléon in 1810 for 137,000 francs—had been set in a diadem worn by Empress Marie-Louise and in the crown of Charles X. The unset diamonds below the buckle are 7 of the 19 so-called Mazarin Diamonds (only a few Mazarins had actually been in Cardinal Mazarin's collection). Tiffany bought 4 Mazarins for a total of 609,000 francs and sold at least 2 of them to Mrs. J. C. Ayer, heiress to her husband's patent-medicine fortune. Right: 1887 auction photograph of Empress Eugénie's "comb" (hair ornament), completed by Bapst in 1856 for the baptism of her son, the Prince Imperial. Tiffany & Co. paid a total of 106,000 francs for 4 diamond pampilles from this comb. Two were sold to Junius S. Morgan, the patriarch of the Morgan banking family, who bequeathed them to his granddaughter, Mary Burns. She remounted the 28 diamonds into the necklace shown on the next two pages.

The Morgan-Burns
necklace and Bapst's
original silver mounting
for the pampilles rest
on the certificate of
authenticity from the
Vente des Diamants
de la Couronne.

OPPOSITE
The Morgan-Burns
necklace.

The early ledgers also confirm that during the 1850s Tiffany & Co. acted as a wholesaler of diamonds to smaller jewelry companies and to watchmakers. There are numerous wholesale transactions with "Bailey & Co.," "Mathey & Brothers" (or "F. L. Mathey"), "Canfield Brothers Co.," "J. E. Caldwell & Co.," and "Samuel T. Crosby."

Bailey & Co. was a leading Philadelphia jeweler located on Chestnut Street from 1848 to 1878. The Matheys (or Mathez) were Swiss-born watchmakers and importers working in New York. Canfield Brothers Co., of 229 Baltimore Street, Baltimore, was a jewelry company founded by Ira and William Canfield, who— like Charles Lewis Tiffany—were originally from Connecticut (as was Joseph Trowbridge Bailey, founder of Bailey & Co.). J. E. Caldwell & Co. is a well-known Philadelphia jeweler founded in 1839 by James Emmett Caldwell, and Samuel T. Crosby was a Boston jeweler who later went into partnership with Henry D. Morse in Morse's Roxbury, Massachusetts, diamond-cutting factory.

On April 24, 1856, the most important diamond parure to date was registered. It consisted of a necklace at $3,353.50 (cost), a bracelet at $825.87, a brooch at $519.00, earrings at $399.25, and three rings at $268.50—a total of $5,366.12. They had been ordered by one of the mid-nineteenth century's most successful and colorful industrialists, revolver king "Colonel" Samuel Colt, who purchased the suite for $8,000 ($170,000 today) to offer his fiancée, Elizabeth Hart Jarvis. "Lizzie" Colt wore her dazzling Tiffany diamonds on their wedding day, June 5, 1856. The wedding was celebrated by the Episcopal bishop of Connecticut in the parlor of the Jarvis family home in Middletown, Connecticut. The distinguished wedding party included Commodore Matthew Perry and possibly Perry's daughter and son-in-law, Caroline Slidell Perry Belmont and August Belmont Sr., who were other notable collectors of Tiffany jewels. The afternoon reception featured a six-foot-tall cake decorated with sugar Colt pistols and rifles. After the reception, the bridal party took the express train to New York, where Colt had hired the entire St. Nicholas Hotel for an even larger reception.

The following morning, the newlyweds sailed for Europe, where they were guests at the coronation of Czar Alexander II, after which they achieved, in America, a form of social celebrity. The event was later described by the U.S. minister to Russia, former Connecticut governor Thomas Seymour, as among the "most magnificent pageants ever witnessed in the world. . . . The display of diamonds and costly attire representing the wealth of Europe were never surpassed" (*Hartford Daily Times*, March 1, 1862). Lizzie Colt undoubtedly wore her Tiffany diamonds to the coronation as well as to other "fetes, balls, and

Paulding Farnham's preliminary studies for pendants with large diamonds. The drawing at top left includes the large rectangular diamond set in Farnham's necklace shown at the 1889 Paris Exposition (see page 73).

parades" (as Sam Colt noted) that made up the weeklong coronation celebra-
tions. She probably also wore the diamond ring that Alexander II's late father,
Nicholas I, had given Colt two years before, as a token of appreciation for the
Colt guns that brought victory to the Russian Imperial Army at the battle of
Tula in 1854.

Three years later, however, another Tiffany client outdid the Colts with
a diamond rivière necklace and a pair of single-stone earrings—registered in
Tiffany's diamond ledger on May 16, 1859, for $6,629.44, and $2,328, respectively.
The buyer, August Belmont Sr., offered the necklace to his wife, Caroline Slidell
Perry Belmont, as a tenth wedding anniversary present. (They had been married
on November 7, 1849, at the Church of the Ascension, which still stands at
Tenth Street and Fifth Avenue in New York.) The necklace broke the 5-carat
standard with a center stone of 5.625 carats, as did the earrings, whose two
brilliants totaled 10.125 carats. The selling price of $12,000 ($260,000 today) set
a record that would not be equaled until after the Civil War. In fact, as late as
November 3, 1870, the *Evening Post* in New York noted with obvious admiration
that "in 1859 Tiffany & Co. received an order for the largest diamond that had,
up to that time, been brought to this country. Its value was $12,000."

The journalist writing for the *Evening Post* may have been referring to the
necklace and earrings discussed above. Or he may have been led astray by the
inflated accounts in the New York press of an October 1859 New York society
wedding where the Tiffany jewels were rumored to have cost $12,000, when in
reality they cost around $10,000. In any case, for a single diamond to achieve a
$12,000 retail price at Tiffany & Co. in 1859, it would have had to weigh around
30 carats—and there were quite simply no 30-carat diamonds retailed in America
in the 1850s.

In New York, as late as the autumn of 1859, jewels were of modest proportion, as witnessed by a much publicized wedding that the press baptized the
"Diamond Wedding" and touted as opening a new epoch of magnificence in
our social history. Tiffany & Co. provided the bridal jewels (see illustrations
on page 15).

The wedding of Don Estéban Santa Cruz de Oviedo of Havana to Miss
Frances Amelia Bartlett of then-fashionable Fourteenth Street, New York, was
celebrated by Archbishop Hughes at old Saint Patrick's Cathedral on Mott Street
in Manhattan at noon on Thursday, October 13, 1859. It was, in the words of the
New York Times, an "epoch in our social history." (The journalist had apparently
not been invited to the Colt's wedding reception at the St. Nicholas Hotel on the
evening of June 6.)

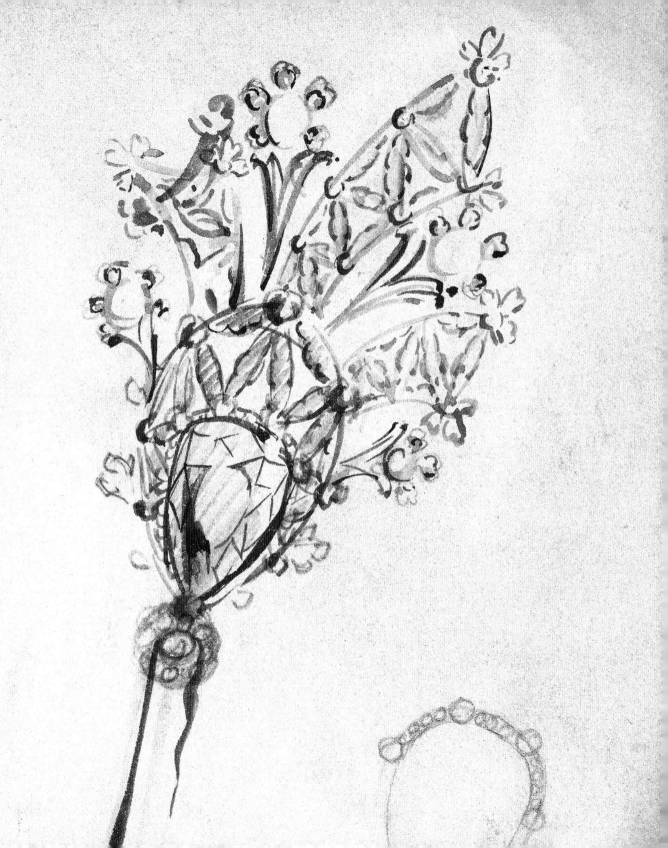

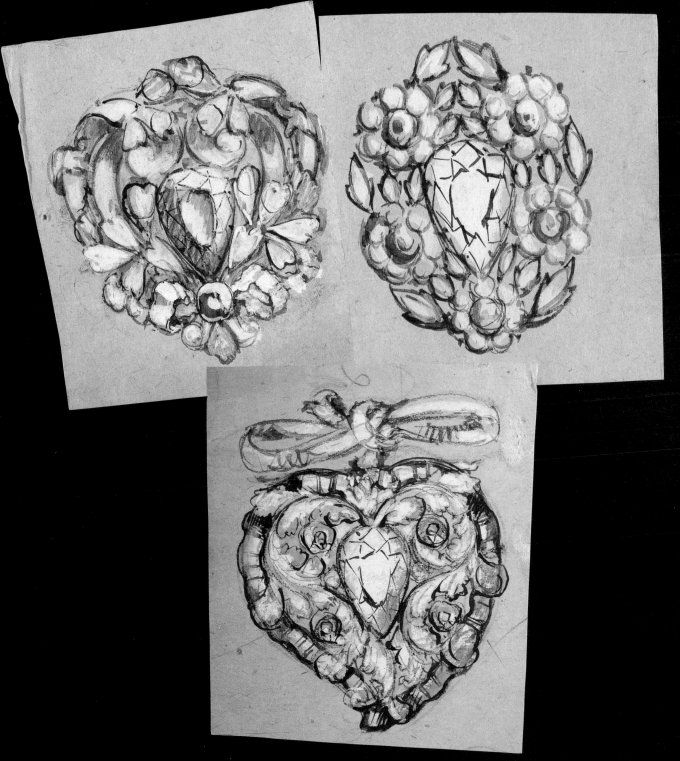

Farnham's study for an eighteenth-century-style pendant brooch with two large cushion-shaped diamonds, probably intended for the 1889 Paris Exposition.

OPPOSITE
Farnham's ca. 1888 study for a diamond hair ornament of the ever-popular stars and crescents of the late nineteenth century.

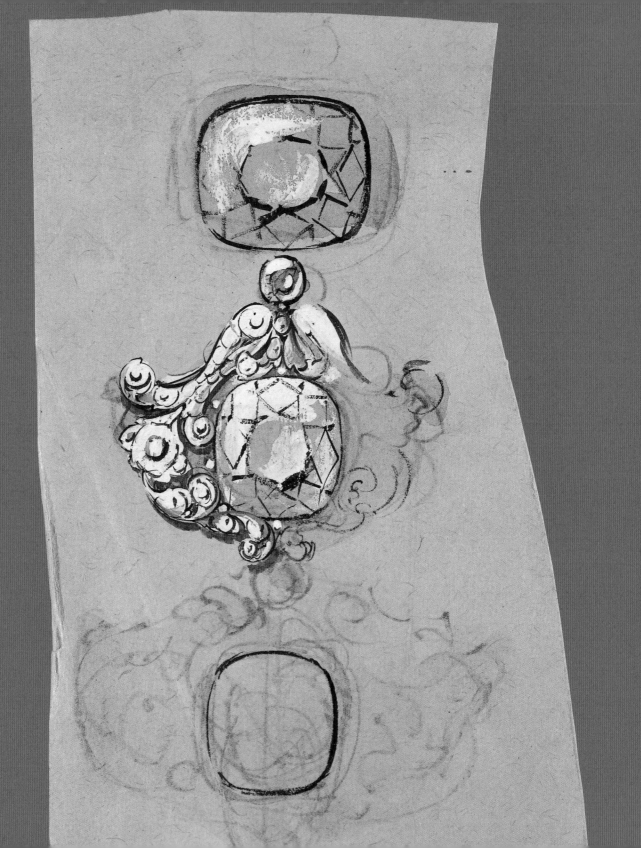

A controversy had raged in the New York press over the fortunes of the Cuban millionaire bridegroom, his age and her youth, and the jewels ordered for the wedding—which were reputed to outshine anything yet seen in New York. The *Times* gave the following description of the Tiffany jewels worn by Miss Bartlett:

About her neck itself a pearl, she wore four rows of shapely orient pearls, looped into a festoon by one slight rib of gleaming diamonds, gathered into the likeness of a knot of love. From this knot depended a single pear-shaped pearl, dipped in diamonds of surpassing lustre and beauty. [The] bride wore two pendant ear-rings formed of diamond soli-taires of great splendor, supporting pear-shaped pearls of proportionate value, capped with brilliants. A brooch, one living Koh-i-noor mountain of light, reposed upon the quiet of a satisfied heart. This enviable orna-ment was all diamonds and pearls, the *briolette* diamond which forms its pendant being regarded by Messrs. Tiffany & Co., by whom the whole parure was imagined and created, as the most unimpeachable single stone in America for beauty and price. The workmanship of all these decora-tions is truly poetic.

Other contemporary accounts made the then-inevitable comparison of the bride to the so-much-admired twenty-nine-year-old Empress Eugénie of France. On October 22, *Frank Leslie's Illustrated Newspaper*, for example, noted that the bride and the empress had "the same style of face, the same drooping of the eyelids, the *spirituelle* aspect of countenance, the same color and manner of wearing the hair." The contemporary illustrations of the bride confirm that every attempt had been made to encourage whatever resemblance to the Empress Eugénie that Miss Bartlett may have had, but the facts surrounding the jewels preclude any realistic comparison to royal jewels, much less to Victoria's Koh-i-noor or to Eugénie's pearls and diamonds, which included the 143-carat Regent.

Tiffany & Co.'s diamond ledger entries of July 19, 1859, the day Oviedo bought the jewels, spell out the realities of the Diamond Wedding. The center stone of the brooch, far from being "one living Koh-i-noor"—with the Koh-i-noor's 105.60 carats—was a small emerald-cut diamond of only 4.57 carats—entered at a cost of $840, and the briolette (an oval-shaped diamond cut in triangular facets), "the most unimpeachable single stone in America for beauty and price," was an even smaller 2.18-carat stone, entered at $155.

As for the pendant earrings "of great splendor," they totaled 3 carats of dia-
monds at a cost of $280, and the pearls cost only $200—a far cry from Empress
Eugénie's favorite diamond-and-pearl drop earrings, purchased in February 1853
from Storr and Mortimer in London, for 35,750 francs (about $7,150). A far cry,
too, from an extraordinary American pink freshwater pearl, later famous as the
Queen Pearl, that Charles Lewis Tiffany had sold—through Tiffany, Reed &
Co.—to the French empress for a large sum, possibly as much as 12,500 francs.
Such, however, was the publicity of the day. It is certain that American—and
Tiffany—jewelry before the Civil War and during Reconstruction was modest
in comparison to the jewelry of foreign courts. The high-flying rhetoric of the
"King of Diamonds" episode of 1848 and the Diamond Wedding of 1859 aside,
the realities were quite down to earth. Even so, with a total cost to Tiffany's of
$6,956.90, plus Charles Lewis Tiffany's usual 33⅓ percent markup, Oviedo must
have paid about $9,276 in total for the diamond wedding jewels (roughly
$212,519 today), a more-than-respectable sum.

The further adventures of Miss Bartlett and her Tiffany diamonds are worthy of note. Widowed in 1870 and subsequently known as the Diamond Widow,
she remarried an obscure German baron and colonel in the Mexican army, Bodo

von Glümer, on September 5, 1882, in a quiet morning ceremony at Trinity Church in New York. Shortly after, on November 21, 1882, Glümer presented her with a new collection of Tiffany jewels worth $8,500 (nearly equal to the value of the collection purchased by Oviedo in 1859). The *New York Times* on September 6, 1882, had noted in a lengthy article titled, "The Bride of the 'Diamond Wedding' Again Married" that "the baroness still retained the diamonds and other gems in their original settings given her by the rich Don." However, on January 27, 1886, the Oviedo jewels (excepting the storied earrings once said to have rivaled the Empress Eugénie's) were returned for $8,700—and finally, on May 16, 1887, the fabled diamond earrings were bought back by Tiffany's for a modest $1,200 from one "Mrs. Bodo von Glümer" as she was bluntly listed in the company's purchase registry. The saga of the Diamond Wedding had reached its conclusion. (Eventually the Glümers moved to Tacubaya, Mexico, where the baroness became an accomplished journalist for Mexico City's daily newspaper *Universal*.)

Eighteen months after the Diamond Wedding, the Civil War began in earnest, on April 12, 1861, and jewels would not have great significance in the American imagination until well after the war ended on April 9, 1865.

Diamond sales did not resume immediately following the war, but they were soon stimulated by the great fortunes made by New Yorkers (and New Englanders) during the war and by the increased availability of diamonds following the 1866 discovery of seemingly limitless deposits in South Africa.

By 1867 imports of diamonds and other precious stones into the United States totaled $1,318,617; in 1868, after the initial impact of availability, the imports dropped off a bit to $1,062,493; in 1869 they went up to $1,997,890; then down to $1,779,271 in 1870. If these seem like small amounts of money today, they were significant then. In 1869 Tiffany & Co.'s total sales in New York were estimated at only $3 million (about $39,480,000 in today's currency).

As diamond sales were once again lively by 1867, Charles Lewis Tiffany went back into the trade of highly pedigreed diamonds so brilliantly explored in 1848. He had by now prospered in the world of gems and jewels to the extent that, upon the sale of one of Europe's greatest jewel collection—that of Hungary's Prince Paul Esterházy, who had died in 1865—Tiffany was able to send an agent to bid on his behalf. The auction was held at 1 P.M. on Friday, March 29, 1867, at Christie, Manson & Woods in London. Bidding against such formidable competitors as the Rothchilds and Queen Victoria's crown jewelers—Sebastian and Robert Garrard—Tiffany's agent carried home a worthy enough amount of Esterházy diamonds (reputedly $100,000 worth, or about $1.2 million today) to

Paulding Farnham's ca. 1889 design for an enameled wild rose brooch, whose flower is centered by an important blue diamond; it was intended for the 1889 Paris Exposition, where Farnham's enameled orchid brooches won international acclaim and a gold medal for jewelry.

FAR RIGHT
Paulding Farnham's ca. 1900 study for a diamond-pavé brooch in the form of a wild tulip.

wild tulip   Europe

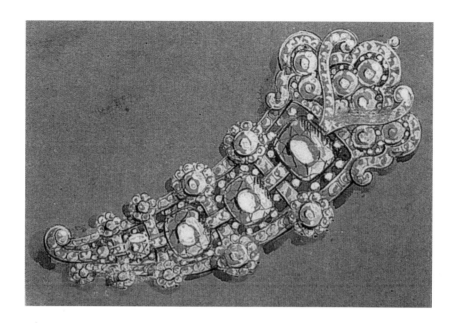

advertise them on June 8 and 9 in the *New York Times* and on June 10 in the *New York Daily Tribune*. The advertisement was headed "The Esterházy Diamonds" and read as follows:

> Tiffany & Co. invite inspection of a remarkable collection of Precious Stones, the larger portion of which, comprising Diamonds from one to five Karats in weight is from the collection of the Prince Esterházy, recently sold in London. Individuals desirous of possessing gems of extraordinary merit and association, should avail themselves of this rare opportunity.

Although it is clear that Tiffany did not yet believe in marketing diamonds of over 5 carats, New Yorkers availed themselves of the "rare opportunity." The Esterházy jewels needed no subsequent advertisements; and the Middle Eastern asymmetries and exotic designs so prevalent in Hungarian jewelry—along with the feathered hair ornaments known as aigrettes so popular in Hungary—began to gain in popularity.

The reversals of fortune in Europe's ruling families continued to provide Tiffany with opportunities to purchase gems of extraordinary merit and association. Various news items in the same June 10, 1867, issue of the *New York Daily Tribune* bear witness to the troubles plaguing the crowned heads of Europe at the

Colorized archival photograph of the Colonial necklace shown at the 1889 Paris Exposition: its pendant featured the 77-carat Tiffany II Diamond (see pages 40–41). *Jeweler's Weekly* reported, "The diamond necklace, of trefoil design, is one of the superb pieces in the collection. The necklace consists of a chain of large diamonds connected by trefoils of smaller stones. In the centre at the front, supported by a scroll of clear diamonds, is a large canary-colored stone. The scroll terminates at each end in a large canary diamond, and from these depends a chain similar in composition and design to the necklace. To this chain two large canary diamonds are pendant, being set in trefoils of clear diamonds at the corners" (June 13, 1889, pp. 41–42). This necklace was not sold at the 1889 exposition, and Tiffany & Co. reset many of its diamonds—including the Tiffany II—in the Canary Diamond Girdle shown at the World's Columbian Exposition held in Chicago in 1893.

Archival photograph of Tiffany & Co.'s most important jewel at the 1889 Paris Exposition, the Hazelnut necklace, priced at $150,000. The pendant's 25.09-carat central diamond had a troubled history: Paris's leading gem dealer, Joseph Halpern, sold it to Turkish sultan Abdul Aziz, who gave it as a wedding present to a member of Egypt's viceregal family. Upon Egypt's bankruptcy in 1875–76, the ousted Ismail Pasha sold it back to Halpern, who ran into financial difficulties of his own and resold it to Tiffany's. This necklace has disappeared: presumably its diamonds were reset in other jewels.

Paulding Farnham's study for a Second Empire–style diamond brooch with a large cushion-shaped diamond at the top and three pampilles; it was intended for the 1889 Paris Exposition.

OPPOSITE
Paulding Farnham's ca. 1888 study for a floriform diamond brooch centered by a round diamond and crowned with an important briolette.

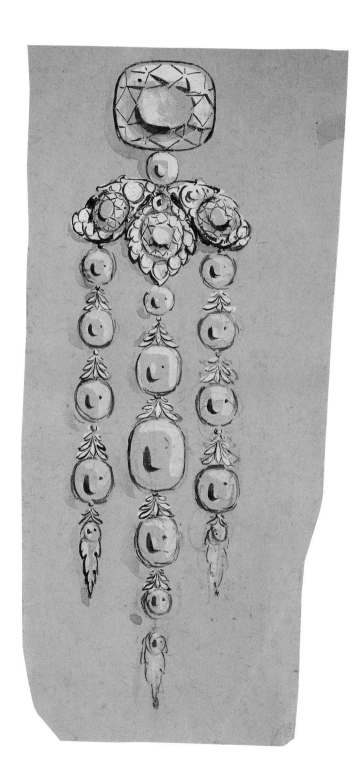

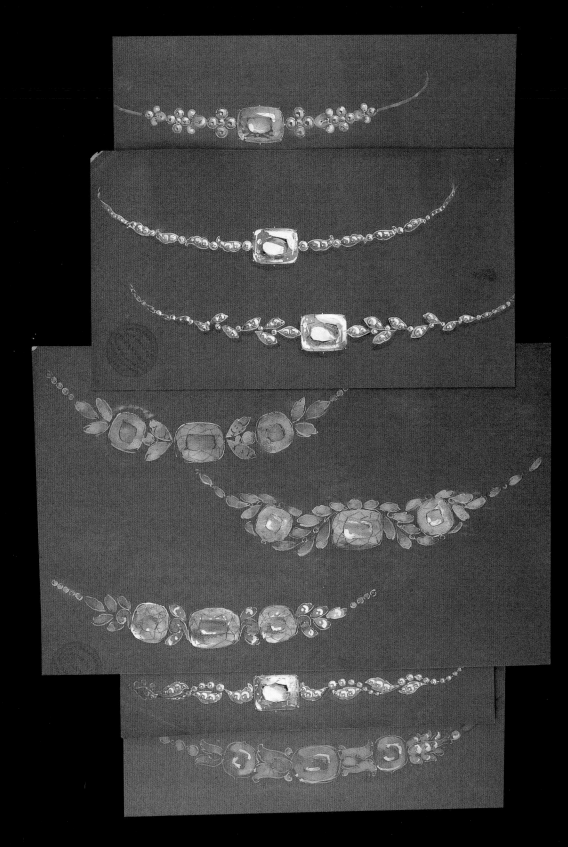

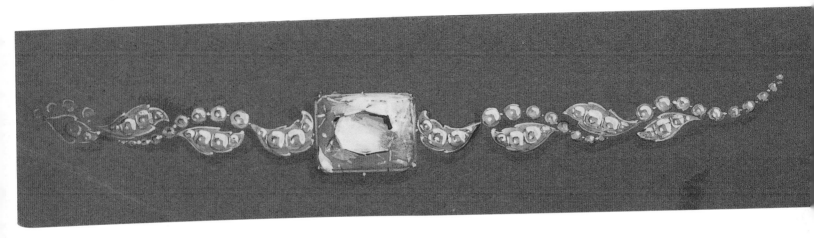

Paulding Farnham's designs for diamond necklaces to be shown at the 1889 Paris Exposition. The design below, centered by a large rectangular diamond, was executed and shown.

Paulding Farnham's
sketches for an aigrette
with a triangular diamond
for the 1889 Paris Expo-
sition.

time. Foremost among these was the capture of Emperor Maximilian in Mexico and the subsequent crowning of Maximilian's older and far luckier brother, Emperor Franz Joseph II of Austria, as King of Hungary. In another item, the *Daily Tribune* noted that "the Poles act honorably and wisely in repudiating the attack made by a fanatic madman upon the Emperor of Russia." The quote refers to an attack by a Polish boy named Berezkowski upon Alexander II while the czar was riding in Napoléon III's carriage at Longchamp. The incident cost France the support of Russia and, coupled with the failure of the French occupation of Mexico, paved the way for the Franco-Prussian War of 1870 and the fall of the Second Empire.

Tiffany & Co. would profit from all these changes—and would also acquire Spanish crown jewels at the sales of jewels belonging to the Empress Eugénie's close childhood friend, the deposed Isabella II of Spain, on Monday, July 1, 1878, and of riches belonging to Isabella's mother, Queen Maria Cristina, on Friday, June 6, 1879. Then in 1887 the firm would make the remarkable purchase at a Paris public auction of about one-third of the actual French crown jewels.

However, the first truly impressive pieces of jewelry that Tiffany & Co. would display were made in Tiffany's own jewelry shop in New York's Union Square, to be shown at the 1876 Centennial Exposition in Philadelphia's Fairmount Park. A march was composed for the occasion by no less than Richard Wagner, and the exposition was opened by President Ulysses S. Grant and Emperor Dom Pedro II of Brazil, on May 10. The first listings in Tiffany & Co.'s catalog were a diamond necklace described as containing "twenty-seven pure white stones of rare perfection and beauty" and a "pair of solitaire earrings of equal quality."

The superb necklace of thirteen perfectly matched pairs of old Indian diamonds, with a somewhat larger diamond at the center, and the earrings were made up of diamonds assembled by George McClure (Tiffany's all-but-forgotten brother-in-law and first gemologist). Together the diamonds weighed 200 carats; they averaged 7.41 carats each. The necklace was priced at $80,000, the earrings at $16,000. They were purchased by Central Pacific Railroad czar Leland Stanford as a present for his wife, Jane Lathrop Stanford, for their twenty-fifth wedding anniversary. The Stanfords would later purchase five sets of jewels that Tiffany had bought at the 1878 sale of the Spanish crown jewels formerly belonging to Isabella II. (Most of these were given by Jane Stanford to finance Stanford University's library in 1902.)

Other major pieces noted in the Tiffany & Co. Philadelphia catalog included a "Peacock's Feather, containing the celebrated 'Brunswick' straw-colored

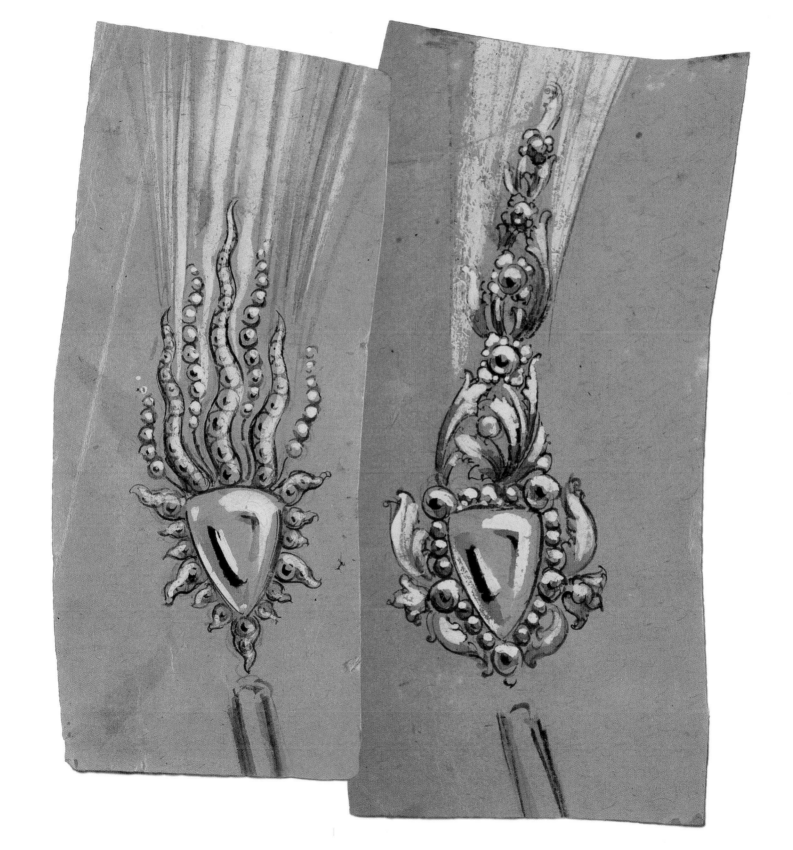

Ca. 1889 drawings.
Top: Tiara centered by
the large pear-shaped,
cinnamon-colored dia-
mond shown by Tiffany
& Co. at the 1889 Paris
Exposition. Center:
Diamond tiara with the
traditional fleur-de-lis
motif. Bottom: Diamond
floral-spray brooch.
These designs were
almost certainly the work
of the unnamed designer
from Paris who began
working for Tiffany's in
New York in late 1870.

OPPOSITE
Archival photograph
of the tiara with the
cinnamon diamond.

diamond." The diamond peacock-feather aigrette, priced at $15,000, attracted the most attention of any jewel at the Centennial. Its 30-carat center stone had been purchased for Tiffany & Co. by Gideon Reed in Geneva, for $8,000, at the 1874 sale of the late "jewel-mad" Duke of Brunswick's collections. Its design had doubtless been influenced by a jewel from Paris jeweler J. F. Mellerio that Tiffany's Paris partner, Gideon Reed, had seen at the 1867 exposition.

The *Jewelers' Circular* of March 1877 described the aigrette, the first great "designed" Tiffany jewel, in detail:

> The feather is intended to be worn as an ornament for the hair. The back shows an elaborate network of gold with numberless interstices, through which the light may reach and add brilliancy to the diamonds. The eye of the feather is formed of a single stone, of peculiar brilliancy and beauty, which has long been known to connoisseurs as the Brunswick yellow diamond. . . . The color is a delicate, lemon yellow, quite unlike the brownish "off-colored" stones of Africa that have become so plentiful within a few years. . . . Immediately surrounding his singularly beautiful gem which, itself, weighs thirty carats, is a circle of diamonds of small size, set in gold of a color nearly like the centre stone, and again, another circle set in deep red gold, the lighter portions of the feather being of platinum. The effect of this combination of colors is highly pleasing, and

though the setting is heavy enough to be perfectly strong, a light feathery appearance is secured by means of numerous joints and springs, which cause a quivering movement at the slightest jar. This matchless jewel contains over six hundred stones, and may well be regarded as a masterpiece of diamond-setting.

The aigrette was also purchased by the Stanfords. An April 30, 1893, story in the *New York Times* included an interview with Mrs. Stanford about her famous jewel collection:

"Though I have possessed this set a number of years," indicating a necklace of yellow diamonds encircled with rubies, emeralds, white diamonds, and sapphires, "it is so conspicuous that I never but once had the courage to wear it, and then it attracted so much notice that I wished it back in its case a thousand times. That is the famous yellow diamond known as the Duke of Brunswick diamond in the centre, and the other stones were selected by Tiffany to match it."

This necklace was delivered to the Stanfords in mid-1878 and cost $76,000. It was among the jewels given to Stanford University in 1902.

Despite all the press, the Brunswick Diamond was totally eclipsed by Charles Lewis Tiffany's 1877 purchase, on McClure and Reed's advice, of the largest canary yellow diamond yet discovered, the Tiffany Diamond. This diamond, greatest of all brought to America in the nineteenth century, was discovered in a Compagnie Française de Diamant du Cap South African mine in 1877 and purchased by Tiffany & Co. as a 287.42-carat rough stone for $18,000—only a little more than twice the price Reed had paid for the 30-carat Brunswick Diamond, whose yellow color was described as merely "straw" rather than "canary." Tiffany & Co. had the stone sent to its Paris branch, where it was cut to a 128.54-carat finished diamond, with an unusual eighty-two facets (plus nineteen small facets on the girdle) instead of the conventional fifty-eight; the cutting was completed in 1878.

Tiffany's displays at the 1876 Philadelphia Centennial had been a sort of dress rehearsal for the upcoming Paris Exposition of 1878, and, given that the United States was in a severe recession in 1876, it was surprisingly successful.

Almost all of the exhibition merchandise had been sold, so by mid-1877 the firm found itself with depleted stocks of gemstones. There was not much left to display except the Tiffany Diamond, which Tiffany was reluctant to show for

Farnham's study for the
Portuguese necklace
shown at the 1893
Chicago Exposition
(see page 107).

OPPOSITE
Paulding Farnham's
study for a diamond-and-
enamel necklace for the
1889 Paris Exposition.

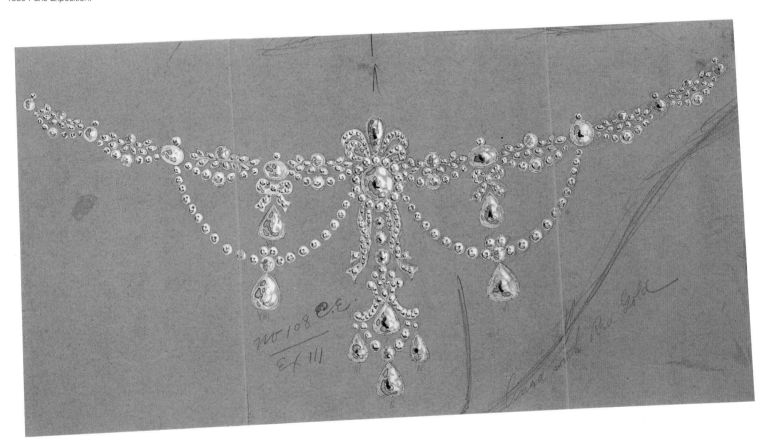

fear that a larger stone would be discovered before the Paris Exposition opened on May 1, 1878. He also knew that the French government would show all of the French crown jewels, including the 140.5-carat Regent Diamond, at the entrance to the show's main pavilion on the Champs de Mars, and it would be impossible to compete with these treasures. Thus the Tiffany Diamond was not to be seen at the Paris Exposition. It was sent to New York and put on display at the Union Square store, and remains on display at Tiffany & Co. (since 1940 at 727 Fifth Avenue) to this day.

Eight years after the exposition of 1878, the French were once again preparing for a world's fair. This one, as is usual in the great battle for one-upsmanship expositions, was set to outshine anything previously attempted. It would commemorate the centennial of the French Revolution.

As preparation for the exposition gained momentum, the French made a surprising announcement in December 1886. After four years of deliberation, the French Senate had decided not to display the crown jewels at the upcoming exposition, as France had done in 1878. Instead, they would sell them.

The report read to the Chamber of Deputies on December 7, 1886, by a deputy named Meullon, sums up the antimonarchist attitude of President Jules Grévy's Republican French government: "A democracy sure of itself and confident of the future has a duty to dispose of luxuries, which are useless and without moral value, and not to leave a considerable sum of money buried unproductively in a basement. This is what should be understood by the numerous pretenders to the throne: and, before arguing over the crown to the great detriment of the country, they could for its advantage argue about the crown jewels in the auction room."

Opposing sentiments were reflected in *The Crown Jewels* by Louis Enault, published in 1884, at the time the government began its drive to "alienate" the jewels: "It appeared regrettable to let these last vestiges of an epoch which had its glories disappear, even if that epoch also had its misfortunes. No one should be so empowered to tear apart the fabric of history. It is in vain that logicians, whose values place algebra before sentiment, tell us that the crown jewels no longer have a reason to exist in a country where there is no longer a crown. Certain instincts of poetry and grandeur, against which all the logic in the world is powerless, persist in a quiet but constant protest which, though it does not translate itself into resounding recrimination is no less real, and will be no less enduring."

The "law of alienation," as it was called, once ratified, was signed by President Grévy and Minister of Finance Sadi Carnot (who would be president at the time of the auction in 1887), and the sale was announced for May 12–23, 1887.

Corsage decoration of 2,500 diamonds designed by Paulding Farnham for the Paris Exposition of 1889. It was priced at 135,000 francs (about $27,000) (see page 94). Overlay of Tiffany's current Victoria necklace and bracelet.

Ca. 1890 studies for a maidenhair-fern–motif necklace and a floriform brooch by Paulding Farnham. The maidenhair fern was a signature motif in his jewelry design—he included it in several of the jewels he designed for the Chicago World's Columbian Exposition of 1893 and the Buffalo Pan-American Exposition of 1901.

OPPOSITE
Another Farnham study for a maidenhead-fern–motif diamond necklace.

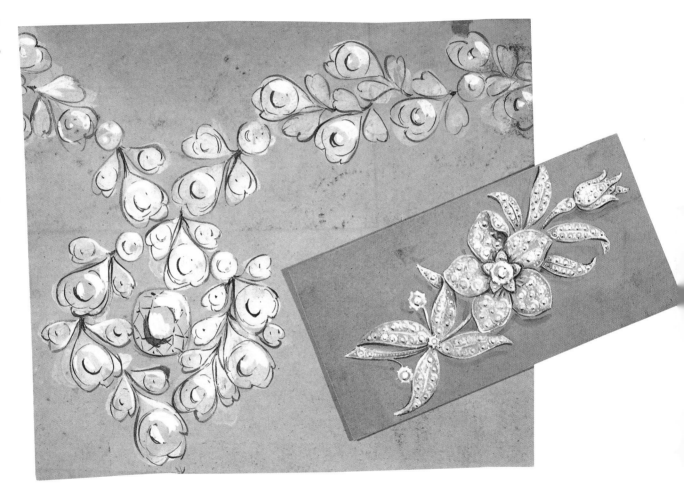

Drawing for a diamond corsage ornament of bow-tied ribbons, ca. 1890.

FAR RIGHT
Tiffany & Co.'s gemologist George Frederick Kunz provided the jewelry department with American pink conch pearls that Paulding Farnham featured in his rosebud-motif designs, some still made to this day. Shown here is a Farnham corsage ornament of diamonds and pink conch pearls placed upon his ca. 1895 drawing for the piece.

The crown jewels, stored in the basement of the Ministry of Finance, were crudely broken into lots to facilitate their sale and photographed by an undistinguished Paris photographer, Berthaud, using uninspired electric lighting. The Ministry of Finance published a catalog using Berthaud's photographs, and only one copy was sent to the United States. It was sent to Tiffany & Co.

The democratic citizens of our country during the Gilded Age of the 1880s felt an irresistible urge to acquire, not "a duty to dispose of luxuries," and were all too willing to have Tiffany & Co.'s agents "argue about the crown jewels in the auction room."

The sale grossed only 6,864,050 gold francs, or $1,324,720, of which Tiffany's purchases accounted for more than one-third, or a total of $487,956.

Empress Eugénie's necklace of four enormous diamond rivières, or ropes of large round stones, completed by Bapst in February 1864 and number ten in the sale, went to Tiffany's for 183,000 francs on May 12. It was the last item on the first day of the public auction in the Louvre's Pavillon de Flore, and it received only one bid. The very next day Mrs. Joseph Pulitzer wore this imperial prize to a Paris party. The vaunting social aspirations of newfound American wealth were fulfilled. The wife of a Hungarian-born New York newspaperman could now own and show herself about wearing Empress Eugénie's jewels.

The world had changed dramatically since late August 1855, when Napoléon III and Eugénie gave a ball in the Hall of Mirrors at Versailles. There Victoria, Queen of England, danced the quadrille with the Emperor of

SCIENTIFIC AMERICAN

[Entered at the Post Office of New York, N. Y., as Second Class matter. Copyrighted, 1891, by Munn & Co.

A WEEKLY JOURNAL OF PRACTICAL INFORMATION, ART, SCIENCE, MECHANICS, CHEMISTRY, AND MANUFACTURES.

Vol. LXV.—No. 3.]
Established 1845.

NEW YORK, JULY 18, 1891.

[$3.00 A YEAR.
WEEKLY.

DIAMOND CUTTING BY HAND AND MACHINE.

Modern diamond cutting is an art which for many generations was practically confined to one city, Amsterdam. In India the natives cut the gems, but they did not follow the rules of shape which have found acceptance with the Caucasian nations. Some twenty years ago the industry was introduced in this country. This was at about the time of the discovery of the South African diamond fields. Mr. I. Herrmann, a jeweler of this city, succeeded in finding among the Dutch who had immigrated to this country a number of diamond workers who from force of circumstances had abandoned their trade and had adopted other occupations.

Diamond Polishing.

consists approximately of two truncated pyramids placed base to base. The line dividing the two pyramids is called the girdle. The upper portion is the crown, with a flat face called the table on top. Below the girdle is the collet. If properly cut, this shape brings out the fullest possible brilliancy of the gem. So important is this quality, that it was deemed advisable to recut the Kohinoor diamond to develop its brilliancy, although many karats were lost in the operation.

Cleaving consists in splitting off pieces of a diamond. By inspection striations can be detected in the rough gem by which its cleavage plane is determined. The stone to be thus

| CLEAVING. | POLISHING ON HORIZONTAL WHEEL. | HAND CUTTING. |

He opened a shop in this city, where much work was done.

The industry s p r e a d more or less, and is now firmly established in several places in the United States. The jewelry firm of Tiffany & Co., of this city, among others, have in operation a shop in which diamonds are cut and polished f r o m the rough, and are recut when the original cutting as performed in Amsterdam or elsewhere has not left them of satisfactory brilliance. The work is in charge of the foreman, Mr. Geo. H. Hampton, to whom we are indebted f o r attentions shown in connection with this article.

The operations of shaping a diamond are three, and may be four, in number: cleaving, cutting, setting and polishing. Each operation is a trade by itself, and very few ever learn to do more than one or two of the four steps. Cleaving is often dispensed with; the other three are necessary. The favorite shape into which every stone of ——— is worked is the ———

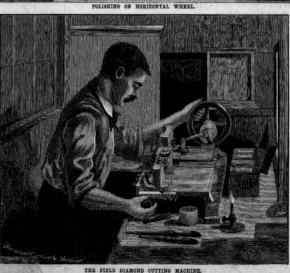

THE FIELD DIAMOND CUTTING MACHINE.

DIAMOND CUTTING BY HAND AND MACHINE.

treated is mounted in cement upon the end of a wooden handle. Upon a second handle a s h a r p-edged fragment such as has been cleaved from another diamond is mounted. The diamond has a little notch made in it by the cleaver pressing and rubbing against it the edge of the fragment. This marks the place for starting the cleavage. A cutting box is used in making this notch. This is shown in the illustration in use for regular cutting. It is a small metal box from whose edge two brass pins or studs rise, against which t h e spindle-shaped handles are pressed in the cutting operation. The cleaver holds a handle in each hand, p r e s s i n g them firmly against the pins and edges of the box. The ends carrying the diamonds project over the box. He then scratches or cuts a notch at the desired place. Next, placing the handle carrying the diamond to be cleaved on its end upon the table, he holds a blunted-edged knife of steel firmly upon the notch and gives the back of the knife a

France and mused on the pale, exquisite beauty of the empress in her light crinolines with long auburn curls flowing down her bare back "à la Bacchante" and wearing her four dazzling new "rivers" of diamonds.

Victoria somehow could see what would come. As she reflected on the strange "dispensations and ways of Providence," she noted in her diary before returning to London the following day, "all is so beautiful here, all seems so prosperous, the Emperor seems so fit for his place, and yet how little security one feels for the future!" History does not record any comment, by either the ex-empress, then living in the country near London, or her lifelong friend Queen Victoria, on the 1887 sale of the crown jewels.

And so by the summer of 1887, not only was Kate Pulitzer dripping in "rivers" of formerly imperial diamonds, but Empress Eugénie's ruby-and-diamond bracelets were inventively clasped about New York socialite Cornelia Martin's ample neck. An 8.48-carat briolette diamond, bought by Louis XVIII in 1818, graced the corsage of former president Andrew Johnson's twenty-nine-year-old former daughter-in-law, the expatriate Katherine May "Bessie" Safford; Josephine Mellon Ayer, the merry widow of "Sarsaparilla King" James Cook Ayer, wore at least two of the Mazarin diamonds. In jewel-crazy San Francisco, Jane Stanford boasted a four-strand necklace made up of French royal pearls; in New York, social queen Caroline Astor adorned herself with some of Empress Eugénie's diamond currant-leaf corsage ornaments.

On the final day of the auction, Tiffany's representative in Paris released the company's official comment to the *New York Times,* which printed it in its entirety the following morning, May 24, 1887. It read, in part: "In making our purchases we took care to pay nothing for historical association. The trade value of the jewels was the sole guiding consideration. The oldest stones are the most interesting from an historical point of view, but they were cut at the time when the lapidary's art had not reached its present perfection, and on that account are less valuable in our sight than the more modern ones."

There was neither poetry nor grandeur in the auction hall—just well-priced merchandise. The 1887 resales of the crown jewels were a fiftieth-anniversary windfall for Tiffany & Co. that put it in a position to devote all its design and gemological supremacy to preparations for 1889, when it would return to Paris triumphant, with the most extraordinary collections of jewels ever produced by an American jewelry house.

In late 1886, Tiffany's new, young, brilliant designer Paulding Farnham was put in charge of preparing the jewelry exhibit for the exposition. He would work with America's greatest gemologist, George Frederick Kunz, on this extraordi-

178 c.e.

bracelet

179 c.e.

THIS DRAWING
RETURNED TO BE
TIFFANY & CO
WHO RESERVE THE SOLE
RIGHT TO ESTIMATE
UPON IT

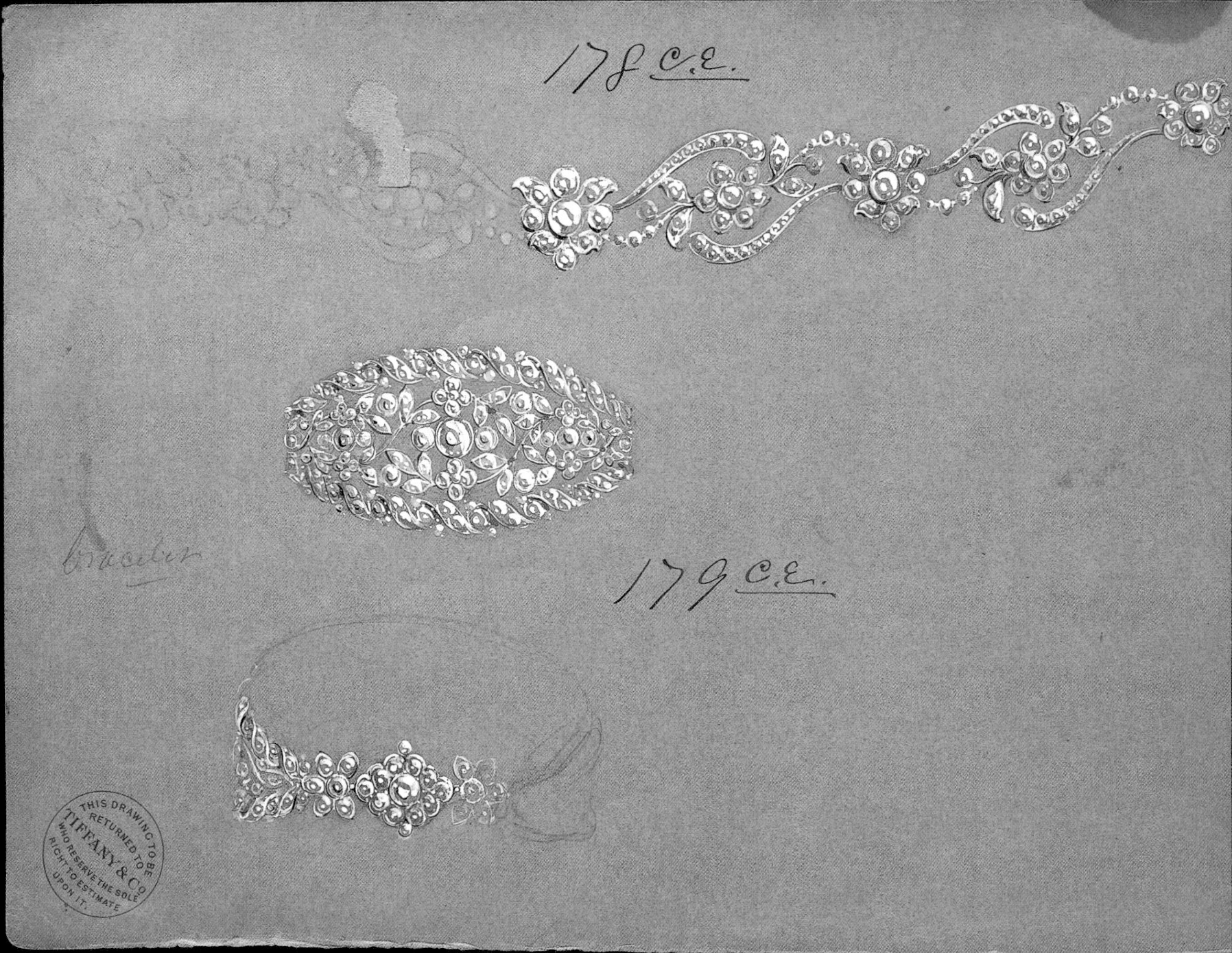

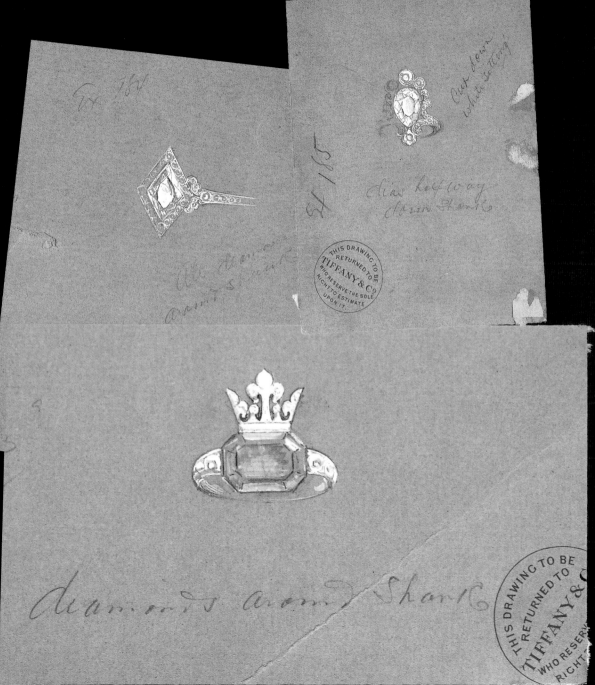

Ex 184

Cut down
white setting

Diaz halfway
down shank

£ 185

All diamond
around shank

diamonds around Shank

nary project. The team was unique in the history of design, jewelry, and gemology, in terms of its talent.

The Paris Exposition of 1889 would be unforgettable. The central and most memorable attraction would be the Eiffel Tower—completed on March 31, 1889, and already a landmark by the time the fair opened on May 6—with its web of iron trusses, lattices, and beams soaring 986 feet into the Paris sky. This instant wonder of the world—part triumphal arch, part cathedral spire—would stand dauntingly above the Champ de Mars and the Seine, asserting France's supremacy in modern design and engineering. The 1889 Exposition Universelle would be a resounding success for the French. There would be 32,250,297 paying visitors; and it would clear a real profit of nearly $2 million, a first in the thirty-eight-year history of international expositions.

It would also be a resounding success for Tiffany & Co., which would carry off six gold medals, including the gold medal for jewelry. To satisfy the Gilded Age's insatiable appetite for eclectic historicism, there were richly conceived jewels in the Louis XIV, XV, and XVI styles.

Tiffany & Co. also displayed a "most conspicuous object" in the form of a *berthe*, or diamond corsage ornament, made of a trellis of two thousand diamonds that went from shoulder to waist. A contemporary journalist described it as "a corsage decoration composed of 2,500 diamonds; it commences from the right shoulder with an immense rosette, falling in diamond lace fringe fully four inches wide, caught in the centre of the bodice by another rosette, and falling still lower to the left side to the waist; it is one of the most superb and import attractions of the Tiffany exhibition and is valued at 135,000 fr." It recalled a trellis of diamonds and imitation pearls Bapst had made in 1864 for Empress Eugénie to wear to a costume ball—purchased for 36,100 francs by Baron de Horn at the 1887 sale of the French crown jewels. Despite their costume jewelry origin and aspect, berthes had gained a certain popularity among the wives of American millionaires following the 1887 sale, and they were proudly worn by the likes of the excessively jeweled Cornelia Martin.

The far finer Colonial necklace in the Tiffany jewelry display paid homage to the Louis XVI jewelry style of 1776 and held at its center the very un-colonial Tiffany II Diamond, a 77-carat yellow stone, which, after the Tiffany Diamond, was the second largest diamond in America; in 1889 it was the largest diamond ever cut in the United States.

Tiffany's most important jewel at the 1889 Paris Exposition was priced at $150,000: the Paris *Herald* euphorically described it as "probably the most extravagant diamond necklace and pendant ever made." The Hazelnut necklace

Paulding Farnham's studies for a diamond-and-pearl necklace, and a diamond-and-pearl corsage ornament for the 1893 Exposition in Chicago.

OPPOSITE
Paulding Farnham's study for a yellow diamond necklace for the 1893 Chicago Exposition, possibly an alternative for the Canary Diamond Girdle.

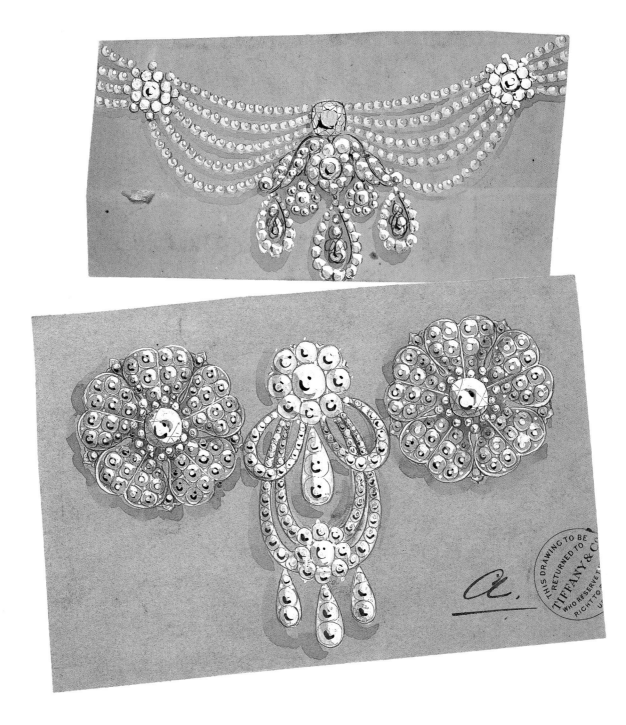

96

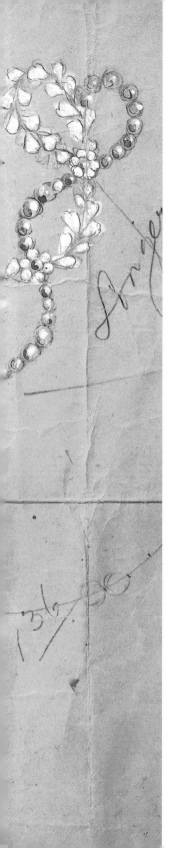

had thirteen diamonds ranging from 5 carats at the back to nearly 20 carats at the front. Each of the thirteen diamonds in the necklace was separated by an American hazelnut-bud diamond and gold rosette. The pendant had a 25.09-carat central stone—priced at $75,000—surrounded by four larger hazelnut-bud rosettes. (At $3,000 per carat, the stone had the highest per-carat price of any diamond offered by Tiffany & Co. in the nineteenth century.) George Frederick Kunz considered it of finer quality than any of the diamonds in the sale of the French crown jewels of 1887—including the Mazarin Golconda diamonds.

The pendant's central stone had a troubled history. It had been purchased by the Turkish sultan Abdul Aziz from Paris's leading gem dealer, Joseph Halpern, as a wedding present for a member of the Egyptian vice-regal family. Upon Egypt's bankruptcy in 1875–76—which resulted in Britain's takeover of the Suez Canal and in Egypt becoming a de facto British protectorate—the ousted Ismail Pasha sold the diamond back to Halpern, who ran into financial difficulties of his own and resold it to Tiffany & Co.

The unlikely name "Hazelnut" came from English essayist Thomas Carlyle's essay on Marie Antoinette's notorious diamond necklace. Written in 1837, "The Diamond Necklace" was published in *Frazer's Magazine*, London. It appeared in New York in 1889, the year Tiffany's diamond necklace was made. In his essay Carlyle describes the seventeen diamonds at the top of the necklace as being "as large almost as filberts [hazelnuts]."

There were other remarkable diamonds in the 1889 Tiffany displays; one noted by *Jeweler's Weekly* was set in a splendid jewel: "A tiara of rare beauty and value contains a very large cinnamon diamond an inch in length. The body of the jewel is composed of small white diamonds, mounted in artistic flourishes and scrolls. The piece is an exceedingly tasteful one in every particular, and is remarkable for its elegance of form and ornamentation no less than for its expensiveness. It is worth $20,000."

Another was a 51.125-carat Tiffany yellow stone, recut in the United States at the same time as the Tiffany II Diamond—and also featured in the Colonial necklace. The August 5, 1887, issue of *Science* noted: "There are 73 facets on the crown or upper side of the stone, and 49 facets on the pavilion or back; and the cutting, which is that of a double-deck brilliant with some of the lower crown-facets divided in two, is quite unique, forming a remarkably beautiful gem" (George F. Kunz). After the Tiffany and the Tiffany II, it was the third largest diamond in America when it was cut in 1883–84 by Charles M. Field, foreman of the Henry Dutton Morse diamond-cutting factory in Boston.

Although largely forgotten today, Henry D. Morse and Charles M. Field

Paulding Farnham's preliminary drawing for a corsage ornament shown at the 1893 Chicago Exposition. Tiffany & Co.'s catalog listed the completed piece, "108. Corsage Ornament. Representing a lattice of maidenhair fern, reaching from the center of the bust to either shoulder, each end forming into a loop, mounted in gold and set with 295 diamonds and 141 pearls."

played leading roles in the history of diamonds in America. In 1860 Morse opened the first U.S. diamond-cutting factory, in Boston, with two diamond cutters from Amsterdam.

Although his first cutters were Dutch immigrants, Morse had the vision of a better-cut diamond, cut for "optimum brilliance" not for optimum weight, as stones were then cut in Amsterdam. "Shopping for diamonds by the carat is like buying a horse by the pound," he told the Boston *Herald* in an early 1875 interview. "Most of the Dutch cutters and polishers are trained to leave the diamond as heavy as possible, and as they invariably work by the piece, the more they finish within a given time the more money they make. Consequently, the work is slighted, the stones thick, clumsy, and ill-shapen, the beauty being sacrificed for weight and profit to themselves. Such is the character of nine-tenths of all the diamonds imported into this country."

Through many years of experiments, and through training American cutters who were not set in the outdated ways of Amsterdam, Morse defined far better proportions for round-cut diamonds—the proportions were close to the "ideal" cut first defined in 1919 by the Belgian mathematician Marcel Tolkowsky, in his treatise *Diamond Design*. (Tolkowksy gave due credit to Morse for his ground-breaking work.)

Morse's factory came to national attention in 1869 when the Dewey Diamond (found in April 1855 by a workman named Benjamin Moore in Manchester, Virginia, on the banks of the James River—the largest diamond until then found in North America) was cut from a 23.75-carat curvilinear octahedron rough into a fine 11.70-carat brilliant. Morse's operation was also greatly aided by the discoveries of his foreman, Charles M. Field, who invented automatic diamond-cutting machines in 1872 and 1875. These, coupled with Morse's own invention of "the Morse Gauge" to standardize cutting angles, led to both time-efficient production and a finer make for round brilliants—a cut that became known as the "early modern" or "American cut."

Morse and Field's first mechanized and truly modern factory opened in 1877—not in time to cut the Tiffany Diamond, which was cut in Paris. However, by 1883, when another celebrated diamond—the Tiffany II—was imported as a rough 124.94-carat stone, it was sent to Boston to be cut by Field. Cutting began on September 29, 1883. When Field finished on January 11, 1884, the stone weighed 77 carats. Kunz purchased it for Tiffany & Co. on February 4, 1884, from its owners, New York importers Louis & Moses Kahn & Co., of 10 Maiden Lane, for $6,500. At just under $90 a carat, it was a bargain price compared to the $266.66 per carat paid for the similarly colored Brunswick Diamond ten years

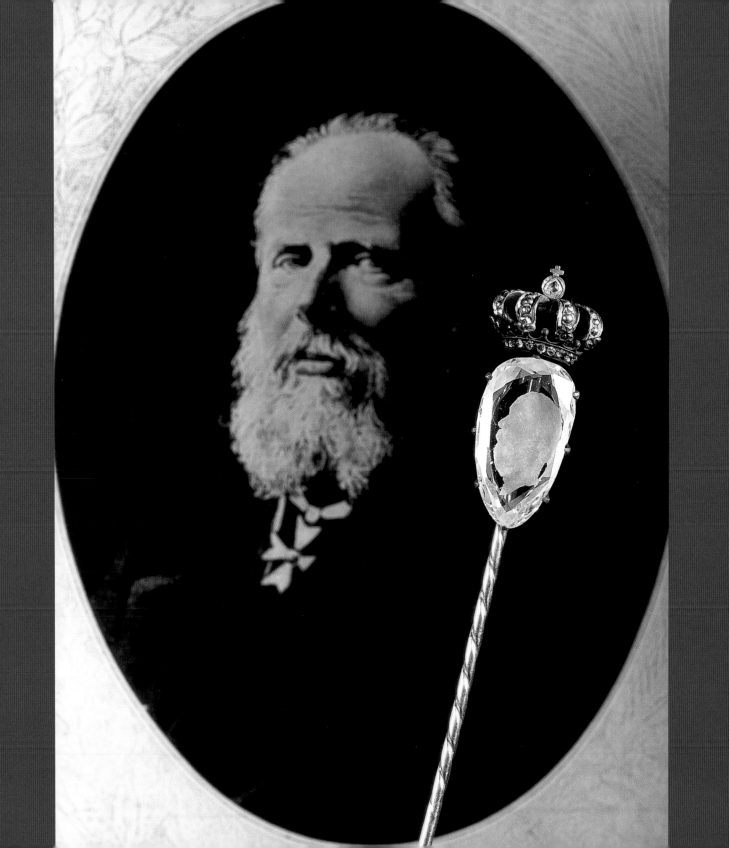

75 my C.E. 7

Plate 64

Ex 211

OPPOSITE
Paulding Farnham's
drawing for a brooch
centered by a 12.75-
carat black diamond,
made for the 1893
Chicago Exposition. This
diamond cost $2,272.50;
the brooch was priced
at $4,000.

LEFT
Eight-carat unset black
diamond from Bahia,
Brazil, shown at the
1893 Chicago Exposi-
tion; it was subsequently
acquired for the Field
Museum.

before. Kunz, who was incontestably the greatest gemologist America had ever produced, recorded his admiration for the Morse factory in the U.S. government's *Minerals Yearbook* of 1883–84 (the year the Tiffany II was cut) and praised its "scientific cutting" methods.

When George Frederick Kunz set up Tiffany & Co.'s own diamond-cutting operation in its Union Square jewelry shop around 1886, it was modeled on Morse and Field's operation and was directed by Boston-trained diamond cutter George H. Hampton, who directed the Tiffany diamond-cutting shop until August 24, 1900.

Jeweler's Weekly of September 28, 1887, sent a journalist to report on the Tiffany cutting operation:

AT THE DIAMOND WHEEL

Now we have reached a small enclosure near the entrance, from which the singing proceeds which tells of the reluctance of the adamantine stone to be beautified, and pushing open the door we find our-selves in the presence of the diamond polishers.

The old Dutch style of cutting diamonds by two tools held in either hand has long been superseded by the ingenious foreman by a machine of his own invention which will rough cut a diamond in less time than is required by any other process.

Szr-r-r sing the polishing-wheels in a high C, as they tear recklessly round in their busy task of making nearly 3,000 revolutions per minute. Each of the heavy "ducks" which rest on the wheel sing in unison, and as the workman takes off one to inspect it we catch a glimpse of a shining point just peering from its bed of white metal. A little more diamond dust is sprinkled on the wheel, and zip, away it whirrs, singing as loudly as ever.

The *Scientific American* issue of July 18, 1891, in a front-page feature on American diamond cutting, again commented on Tiffany's well-established shop that was then cutting stones for jewels to be shown two years later at the Chicago World's Columbian Exposition:

> The jewelry firm of Tiffany & Co., of this city have in operation a shop in which diamonds are cut and polished from the rough, and are recut when the original cutting as performed in Amsterdam or elsewhere has not left them of satisfactory brilliance. The work is in charge of the foreman Mr. Geo. H. Hampton. A machine has been introduced which is in constant operation in the Tiffany shop. It is essentially a planning machine.
>
> The machine is the invention of Charles M. Field, of Boston, Mass., and is only the third in use. It does not entirely supplant hand cutting, as much trimming and shaping of the girdle or outline of the stone is still done by hand.

By 1885 there were already ten other diamond-cutting operations in America besides Morse's, but his was the largest, with thirty cutters and twenty-four of Field's steam-powered polishing wheels. (Still a modest operation compared to Coster's in Amsterdam, which employed around four hundred workers.) Boston's leadership, however, in the American diamond-cutting industry was short-lived. The 1870s saw a great influx of Dutch immigrant cutters to New York, and by 1880 there were sixteen diamond-cutting firms in New York and only three in Boston. The New York immigrant cutters reverted to the old cut-for-weight methods of their native Amsterdam, while Tiffany & Co.'s diamond-cutting shop, under George Frederick Kunz's leadership, produced stones cut to Charles M. Field's standards for the "early modern" or "American cut"—and so gained an edge of superiority in the New York jewelry trade. The white diamonds in the Hazelnut and Colonial necklaces shown at the 1889 Paris

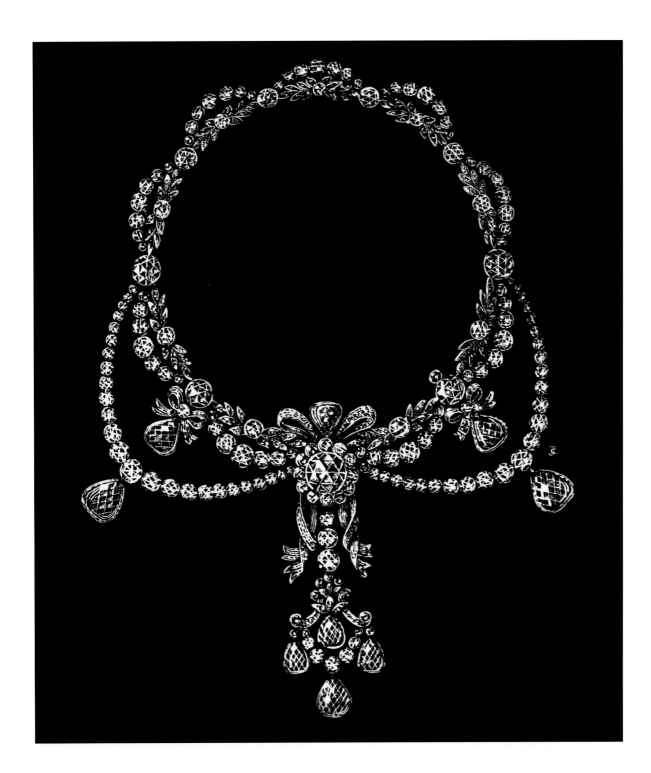

OPPOSITE
Ivy necklace of diamonds set in gold-backed silver, designed by Paulding Farnham ca. 1902–4. It originally had a frame so that it could be worn as a tiara.

LEFT
Illustration of the Portuguese necklace shown at the Chicago Exposition, from Henry Vever's *Exposition Internationale de Chicago* (Paris: Imprimerie Nationale, 1894, p. 57). *Jewelers' Review* commented, "The Portuguese diamond necklace . . . represents all the different styles of cutting in Tiffany & Co.'s workshops, such as brilliant, roundel, pierced and faceted like beads, briolette with lozenge facets, pear-shaped drops, table diamonds and other forms of cutting." Set with 550 diamonds, it was priced at $4,000. Tiffany's catalog states that diamonds were set in a "new diamond metal." The company kept the metal's composition secret at the time: it was probably the alloy of platinum and iridium that became standard in the jewelry industry.

Exposition, are "American cut," which strongly suggests that they were cut in Kunz's new Tiffany & Co. diamond-cutting shop.

In the *New York Herald* of August 4, 1889, Tiffany & Co.'s vice president, Charles Thomas Cook, clarified this point: "In our exhibit in Paris many of the gems mounted in the jewelry are of our own cutting, but in order to show the perfection diamond cutting has attained in the United States we exhibit a small collection of unset diamonds of our own cutting, and in the mineralogical collection, also, all the cut gems are specimens of our lapidary work. Over there they are envious of the American work and said we employed Frenchmen to do it. Therefore we have had to put up a sign that everything has been executed by American workmen under American training. In 1892 we shall show them something even more astonishing."

It is interesting to note that a surviving engraving of the diamond necklace purchased by Leland Stanford at the 1876 Philadelphia Centennial Exposition shows the twenty-seven "pure white stones of rare perfection and beauty" and "pair of solitaire earrings of equal quality"—as the Tiffany catalog described them—to be old European-cut stones that had clearly not been sent to Morse for recutting (as George Frederick Kunz would have done a few years later). Kunz did not take over the gemology department from Charles Lewis Tiffany's brother-in-law George McClure until 1879; and although McClure was considered to be one of the leading diamond experts in America in his day, he does not appear to have found fault with Amsterdam's cutting methods in 1876.

By the time of the World's Columbian Exposition of 1893—the greatest of all American world's fairs—George Frederick Kunz was generally acknowledged as the globe's leading gemologist, and his display of Tiffany diamonds at the exposition was (along with the first Ferris wheel) a wonder of the day.

Tiffany & Co. excelled at the Chicago exposition, receiving no less than fifty-six prizes. The firm was unrivaled in its display of jewelry. At the display's center, the main jewelry case dazzled visitors with the popularly named "Million-Dollar Diamond Group." Both of America's largest diamonds, the Tiffany Diamond and the lesser Tiffany II Diamond—the latter plucked from the Colonial necklace of 1889 and now set in a girdle, or belt, of yellow diamonds and gold chains—were on display. So was a curious diamond that Tiffany & Co. had purchased at the Paris Exposition of 1867, a pear-shaped stone engraved with an intaglio portrait of King William III of the Netherlands—an engraving that had taken an Amsterdam diamond cutter (Mr. C. M. deVries at the Coster factory) five years to complete. (It was later purchased for the gem collection of Chicago's Field Museum of Natural History, where it remains today. The fate of the Tiffany II Diamond is unknown after its final appearance at the 1893 Chicago fair.)

The August 1893 issue of *Jeweler's Review* commented as follows on the Tiffany display:

Enthusiasts, watching the endless throngs crowding around the Tiffany diamonds at the Fair, have declared that were any single exhibit to be chosen for a special grand prize as the greatest international exposition the world has ever seen, the Tiffany diamonds would know no rival. The general character of the jewelry exhibit made by the firm reveals the most exhaustive study of all the earlier periods noted for their artistic productions; there are suggestions of the Giardinetto jewelry, the old Italian style of the fourteenth and fifteenth centuries, old Hungarian, Russian, Turkish, Spanish, Egyptian, Portuguese, Viking, Grecian, Siamese, East Indian, Burmese, Javanese, Japanese, and the French of the Renaissance, the Empire, the Louis', and other periods.

The pièce de résistance is of course the famous "Tiffany Diamond." This stone is truly the "Eiffel Tower" of the Tiffany Exhibit. It is mount- ed upon a pinnacle in the great case of diamonds and by an ingenious mechanical contrivance makes a double revolution one of which draws out all the reflections and colors of the wonderful stone and with the other revolution if sheds its lustre like a search light at intervals upon all the other gems in the case and in circling around affords everyone a good opportunity to see it. The next largest is a light yellow stone weighing 77-carats, and like the large one, is a perfect stone.

Tiffany & Co.'s dazzlingly extravagant display of diamonds at the Chicago Exposition of 1893 was the crowning achievement of Charles Lewis Tiffany's then forty-five-year reign as the King of Diamonds—which began in 1848 when total diamond and other precious stone imports into the United States were far short of the $1-million mark.

The U.S. Bureau of Mines first kept track of diamond imports beginning in the fiscal year of June 30, 1866–June 30, 1867, when diamond imports reached $1.2 million. The total fell to just under $1 million in 1868. By 1869, as South African diamonds that had been discovered in 1866 appeared on the market, the figure jumped to $1.8 million.

Tiffany & Co.'s sales in 1869 were approximately $3 million, which would indicate (taking into account Tiffany's 33⅓ percent markup) that the cost of

TIFFANY & CO
GOLD & SILVER SMITHS
UNION SQUARE
NEW YORK

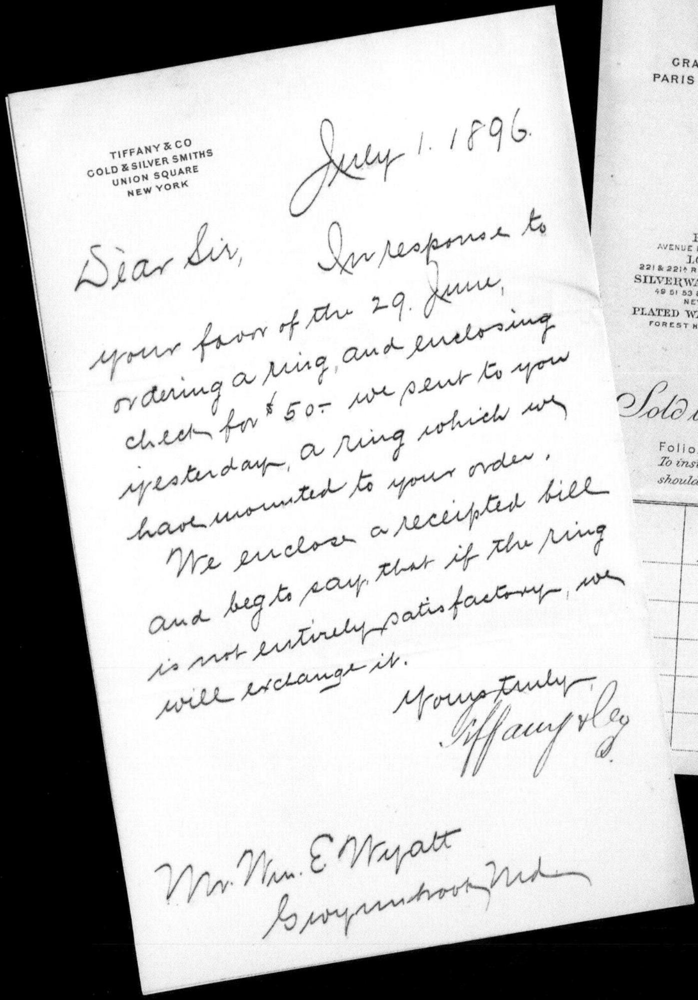

July 1. 1896.

Dear Sir, In response to your favor of the 29. June, ordering a ring, and enclosing check for $50.– we sent to you yesterday, a ring which we have mounted to your order.

We enclose a receipted bill and beg to say, that if the ring is not entirely satisfactory, we will exchange it.

Yours truly
Tiffany & Co
S.

Mr. Wm. E. Wyatt
Gwynnbrook, Md.

GRAND PRIZE
PARIS EXHIBITION
1878.

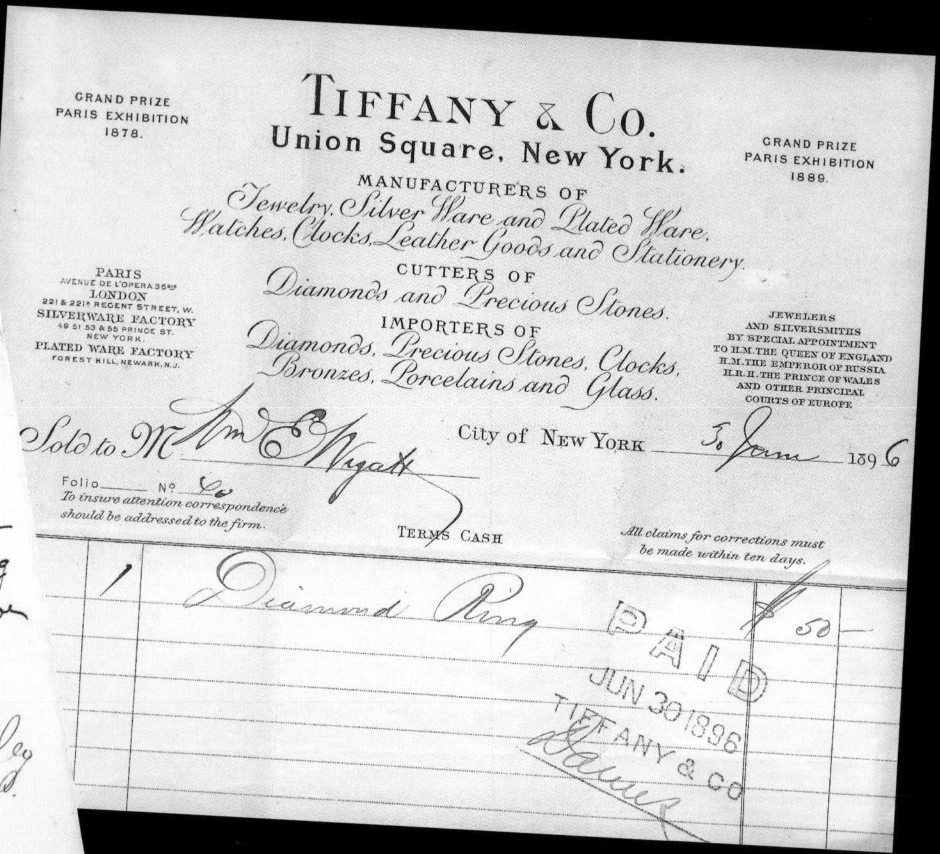

TIFFANY & Co.
Union Square, New York.

GRAND PRIZE
PARIS EXHIBITION
1889.

MANUFACTURERS OF
Jewelry, Silver Ware and Plated Ware,
Watches, Clocks, Leather Goods and Stationery.
CUTTERS OF
Diamonds and Precious Stones.
IMPORTERS OF
Diamonds, Precious Stones, Clocks,
Bronzes, Porcelains and Glass.

PARIS
AVENUE DE L'OPERA 36bis
LONDON
221 & 221a REGENT STREET, W.
SILVERWARE FACTORY
49 51 53 & 55 PRINCE ST.
NEW YORK.
PLATED WARE FACTORY
FOREST HILL, NEWARK, N.J.

JEWELERS
AND SILVERSMITHS
BY SPECIAL APPOINTMENT
TO H.M. THE QUEEN OF ENGLAND
H.M. THE EMPEROR OF RUSSIA
H.R.H. THE PRINCE OF WALES
AND OTHER PRINCIPAL
COURTS OF EUROPE

Sold to Mr Wm E Wyatt City of NEW YORK 30 June 1896

Folio ___ No. 60
To insure attention correspondence should be addressed to the firm.

TERMS CASH

All claims for corrections must be made within ten days.

1	Diamond Ring	$ 50–

PAID
JUN 30 1896
TIFFANY & CO

1    $140.

2    $50.

3    $80.

·TIFFANY & CO·
·UNION SQUARE·
·NEW YORK·

5    $170.

6    $235.

7    $285.

June 25th 96

OPPOSITE

A Tiffany solitaire diamond ring advertisement from 1896, with handwritten prices. It shows the pronged Tiffany Setting created under Charles Lewis Tiffany's direction in 1886; it soon became standard in the jewelry industry and remains standard today.

LEFT

Two views of a ca. 1890 solitaire ring with a 3.19-carat European-cut diamond in an early example of the classic six-prong Tiffany Setting.

goods was $2 million. Tiffany's traditional, nineteenth-century sales mix would further suggest that at least 40 percent of the sales were in diamonds ($800,000 at cost), accounting for close to one-half of all diamonds imported into the United States. The King of Diamonds had little serious competition—a situation that continued until 1893, when the financial panic of that year and the ensuing recession (its severity was of depression proportions) caused the demand for diamonds to fall by nearly 50 percent and to remain at that level for the next four years. That four-year period also saw the U.S. government raise the import duty on diamonds, both cut and rough, to 25 percent—a move which seriously damaged America's role in the diamond industry. (The tariff was repealed in 1898.)

It was an extraordinary forty-five-year period in the economic, cultural, and social growth of the United States, where Charles Lewis Tiffany ruled as King of Diamonds. During that period he provided the diamond jewels that commemorated the weddings and anniversaries and the achievements of legions of America's most prominent citizens. These were regularly chronicled in the New York press by features which paint a wonderfully romantic and glamorous—and often inspiring—portrait of America in the last half of the nineteenth century, the "Gilded Age."

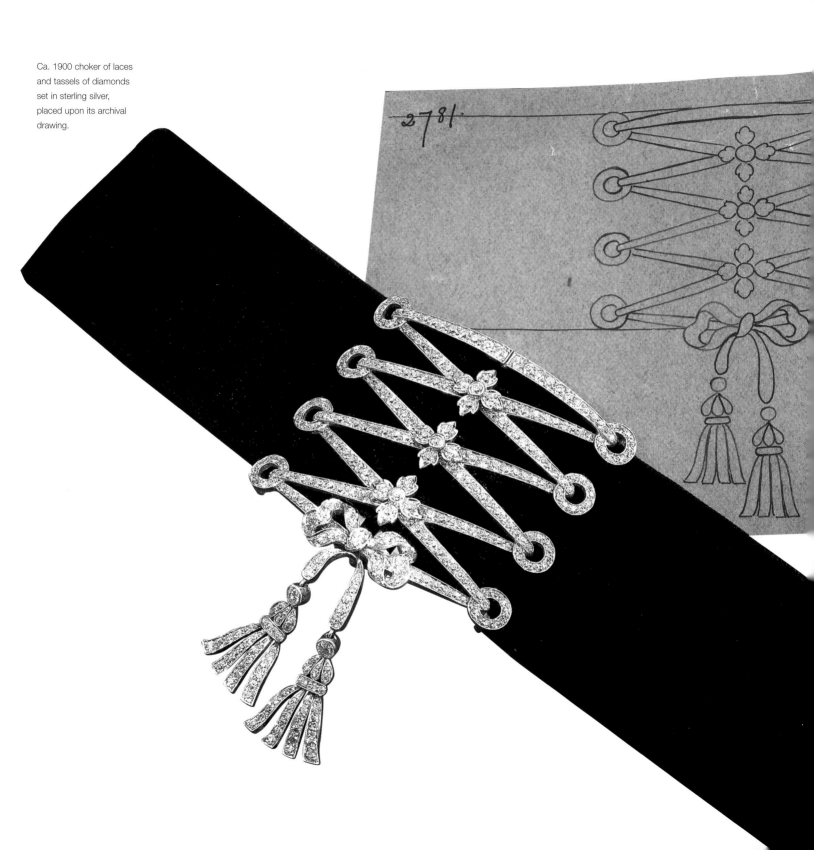

Ca. 1900 choker of laces
and tassels of diamonds
set in sterling silver,
placed upon its archival
drawing.

Following the much publicized weddings of "Colonel" Samuel Colt to Elizabeth Hart Jarvis on June 5, 1856, and of Don Estéban Santa Cruz de Oviedo to Frances Amelia Bartlett on October 13, 1859, the next great parade of Tiffany diamonds was at the spectacular ball held for Prince Edward of Wales at the Academy of Music on Fourteenth Street, on the evening of October 12, 1860 (see illustration on page 16). Mrs. Edwin Denison Morgan, wife of New York's newly elected forty-nine-year-old railroad millionaire governor (and chief fundraiser for Abraham Lincoln's 1860 presidential campaign), opened the dance with the prince to the music of a Strauss quadrille. The *New York Times* reported as follows on October 13 on what may have been the most splendid party ever thrown in New York:

The wealth of flowers lavished upon corridors, galleries, box-fronts and doorways was tropical for variety of hue, and Arabian for odors of beatitude. All that music could do to enchant an aromatic atmosphere with melody, the most superb bands procurable in America abundantly did. The Prince of Wales, who apparently has Queen Elizabeth's passion for dancing, made his entrée punctually at ten o'clock, armed and equipped as the Committee had kindly directed, in "full evening dress," with all the noblemen and gentlemen of his suite. The stately Mrs. Morgan, in a cloud of crepe alive with diamonds, was at her post, prepared to open the ball as became the queen regnant of the Empire State, with the young heir of England.

Velvet and dowagers have this merit that they imply diamonds, and the implication on this occasion was verified in fact. One might almost have fancied himself in St. Petersburg [a reference to the coronation of Czar Alexander II on September 7, 1856]. The distribution of diamonds was so wide that glanced at from a distance, they made a most effective element in the *coup d'oeil* of the ball. One splendid *rivière* which recently astounded the city in the cases of Tiffany was most charmingly displayed upon the graceful beauty of Mrs. Belmont, and shone afar even over the glittering crowd, from her place on the right of the stage.

There passes before us, as the names of the queens of the evening float up in our memory, such a kaleidoscope of azure colors and cloudy laces, and gleaming jewels, that it seems idle to attach mortal names to such a phantasmagoria of brilliant effects. We have already spoken of Mrs. Morgan and her diamonds, and of Mrs. Belmont and her diamonds. We might go on in the same way, with perfect truth, to speak of half the ladies of New York and their diamonds. Diamonds went aside, for they were rather the rule than the exception of the evening. Mrs. Robert B. Minturn contrived to throw them into the shade with a waving head-dress of ostrich feathers, altogether courtly and precious, without reference to its implied compliment to the Prince and his plume. Mrs. Aspinwall was also notable in a glory of blue moiré antique, powdered with jewels, and Mrs. Grinnell, in black moiré antique, decidedly declined the condition of a "dowager." A delicate shade of mauve-color, flounced with laces, till they seemed a sort of frosted amethyst, and ici-cled over with glittering diamonds, varied the expanse of more familiar tints. Mrs. Hamilton Fish, and the muse of the drama, in the person of Mrs. Hoey, of Wallack's Theatre, were conspicuous patronesses of this pleasing hue.

The *Cosmopolitan Art Journal*'s December issue reported:

Messrs. Tiffany & Co., the jewelers, say over one hundred and fifty thousand dollars worth of jewels were ordered during the ten days preceding the grand ball given the Prince at the Academy of Music, in this city.

Tiffany's diamond ledgers indicate that, as with almost all mid-nineteenth-century journalism, the *Cosmopolitan Art Journal*'s account was given to certain exaggeration. However, that the stars of America's monied society spent fortunes on diamonds at Tiffany & Co.'s Broadway store in the seven years preceding the Civil War is a matter of record. That they would go on to spend even greater fortunes on diamonds at Tiffany & Co.'s newer Union Square store in the 1870s, 1880s, and 1890s, is also a matter of record.

Tiffany & Co.'s clients for its fine diamonds before the Civil War had been an intriguing mix of old American society, such as Mrs. Hamilton Fish; new American society, such as Mrs. August Belmont Sr. and Mrs. Edwin D. Morgan; and well-married adventuresses, such as the extravagant actress Josephine Shaw Hoey.

If the fortunes of many of Tiffany & Co.'s earlier diamond clients came from shipping—as was the case with the Charles Morgans, the John Hoeys, the Nathaniel McCreadys, and the Moses Brown Iveses—those of its post–Civil War clients came from the railroads, which brought untold prosperity to the United States from the end of the Civil War until the depression of 1893.

RIGHT AND OPPOSITE
Lavish Louis XVI–style
ca. 1900 necklace of
bezel-set diamonds set
in platinum and 18-karat
gold; it can be divided
into a shorter necklace
and a bracelet. The
necklace was made for
Ellen Garretson Wade
(1859–1917), whose
husband, Jeptha Homer
Wade (1857–1926), was
an industrialist and gem
collector who specialized
in rare colored diamonds;
he was advised by
Tiffany gemologist
George Frederick Kunz.
His collection is now at
the Wade Gallery in the
Cleveland Museum of
Natural History.

Purchases by the Vanderbilts and by Alexander Johnston Cassatt on the East Coast mixed with those of the even more extravagant "big four" of the Central Pacific Railroad: Charles Crocker, Mark Hopkins, Leland Stanford, and Collis Potter Huntington of the west coast. (Chicago railroad car manufacturer George M. Pullman and New York streetcar magnate and secretary of the navy William Collins Whitney also joined in.)

Predictably, the purchases of the old guard of American society were modest in comparison to the fortunes spent by the newly rich of the age of railroads. When James Roosevelt married William Astor's daughter Helen on November 18, 1878, he presented her with a solitaire diamond ring purchased from Tiffany & Co.'s Union Square store on October 29, 1878, for a mere $1,000. But a year later, when railroad czar Collis Huntington bought his wife, Elizabeth Stoddard

Huntington, Tiffany diamonds to celebrate their twenty-fifth Christmas together, he selected an $8,500 necklace.

The Vanderbilts outdid Huntington on March 22, 1882, when Frederick William Vanderbilt purchased an even larger Tiffany diamond necklace for his wife, Louise Holmes Anthony Vanderbilt, for $19,600. (To put things in perspective, this was $1,600 more than Tiffany & Co. had paid for the Tiffany Diamond five years earlier.)

Following the 1866–67 discovery of vast diamond deposits in South Africa, diamonds obviously became more plentiful and less expensive on the world market; however, Tiffany's principal diamond expert, George McClure, considered African stones inferior to Indian (Golconda) stones and to Brazilian stones (which Tiffany clearly dealt in). As late as December 20, 1874, he made

his (and therefore Tiffany's) position clear in a lengthy text published in the *New York Times*:

DIAMONDS

The discovery of diamonds in South Africa and the consequent throwing on the market of quantities of stones, mostly of inferior qualities has so depressed prices that they are now lower than at any time since 1818.

First quality white stones, such as are known as "First Water" and the best of the second quality, are now in price far below their real value. At these low prices we have added largely to our stock of these grades, and now offer the largest stock of selected stones in this country.

Purchasers wishing to select from unset stones will find every size and weight in general use and will receive our best assistance and advice in making selections.

Fine old India stones alone have been but little affected. They are rarely met with, and only in the hands of connoisseurs, be they dealers or not, who, knowing their rarity, are not willing to part with them at less than full value.

During extensive dealings for many years, we have collected and always add to our collection of this class of stones when opportunity offers so that we are generally prepared to furnish specimen stones.

The market is full of the lower grades of African stones, and many are tempted to purchase them on account of their seeming low prices, but we advise our customers to avoid them as it is difficult to name a price at which they would be cheap.

TIFFANY & CO.
DIAMOND MERCHANTS
UNION SQUARE, NEW YORK

The arrival of George Frederick Kunz at Tiffany & Co. changed all this. Kunz was something of a child prodigy in the world of gemology, already collecting and exchanging stones with other gem collectors in 1870 when only fourteen years old. In 1875, at nineteen, he sold a collection of gemstones to the University of Minnesota (for all of $400). The next year he made his first sale (a green tourmaline) to Charles Lewis Tiffany. Tiffany was impressed with the young gemologist and hired him in 1877 to assist McClure.

Kunz, as well as Tiffany's Paris partner Gideon Reed, must have had a hand in convincing Charles Lewis Tiffany to buy the Tiffany Diamond (an African stone) in 1877; and, as McClure's eyesight was failing, it was Kunz who supervised the stone's cutting in 1878. George Frederick Kunz took over as Tiffany & Co.'s vice president and gem expert in 1879, at the tender age of twenty-three. Then in 1880 George McClure's poor eyesight forced his retirement from gem purchasing, and McClure's assistant diamond expert, Charles L. Seale, also withdrew—leaving Kunz in full command of gemology at Tiffany & Co., where he remained for fifty-two years, until a few days before his demise on July 29, 1932.

Kunz, unlike McClure, was enthusiastic about the new and abundant supply of diamonds from South Africa—and excited about colored diamonds as well. The purchase and cutting of the 128.54-carat intense yellow Tiffany Diamond had been a brilliant success. The finished stone was finer and deeper in color than the 125-carat Brazilian Star of the South that Malhar Rao, the Mahratta of Baroda, had purchased for four hundred thousand francs (about $80,000) nearly a decade before—following its exhibit at the Paris Exposition of 1867. (The price of the Star of the South was over four times that which Charles Lewis Tiffany paid for his great diamond.)

Kunz's purchase of the Tiffany II Diamond in 1884 and of the fine yellow 51.125-carat stone at about the same time, along with the other sizable yellow diamonds displayed in the Colonial necklace in 1889 and reset in the Roman Girdle of 1893, bear out his fondness for colored diamonds. On the other hand, there is only one recorded sale of a colored diamond of any size on Tiffany's books during George McClure's tenure—a quite unremarkable yellow brilliant of 3.31 carats set in a ring numbered 1809 and registered on August 8, 1853, for $130.

Shortly after joining Tiffany & Co., George Kunz convinced the firm's most extravagant diamond collector, Mrs. Charles Morgan—widow of a shipping tycoon—to purchase a yellow diamond for $1,500 ($26,000 in today's currency). The following year, on March 11, 1882, he sold California's Mrs. Leland Stanford a pair of yellow diamond solitaire earrings for $1,550 ($27,000 today) and on December 14, 1882, he sold a rare green diamond ring to Mr. Charles J. Osborn for $4,500 ($80,000 today). In 1885, the November 6 issue of *New York Town Topics* described as follows Tiffany & Co.'s jewels:

The particular feature of fall styles is the use of colored diamonds. The colored diamonds are not by any means "off-color" stones, which means those of an indifferent tint, whether white or otherwise, but of deep and

OPPOSITE
Farnham's drawings for
the pendant.

LEFT
Necklace with a multicol-
ored diamond pendant
designed by Paulding
Farnham in the "Por-
tuguese" style about
1895–1900. Farnham
introduced this style with
an important diamond
necklace containing
seven briolette pendants,
shown at the 1893
Chicago Exposition
(see page 107).

Archival photograph of a Spanish Renaissance–style diamond and enameled gold necklace; it was the only jewel by Paulding Farnham shown by Tiffany & Co. at the 1904 St. Louis Exposition. The chain was ornamented with enameled figures, and the diamond pendant could be divided into smaller pendants and a pair of earrings. Gustav Stickley, the leader of the American Arts and Crafts Movement, wrote in 1904, "[It] consists of a pendant and chain, designed in a strictly historical style, and reproducing a parure that might have been worn by the queens of Charles V, Francis I, or Henry VIII. The rose-cut diamonds and clustering brilliants are correctly used after the manner of the sixteenth century, and the work as a whole is intended as a tour de force of craftsmanship; great difficulties having been met in maintaining the delicate proportions of the figures of the links throughout the process of enameling" (*The Craftsman,* October 1904, p. 181). The necklace was broken up around 1915, and the top and bottom center elements were incorporated into a pearl *sautoir* made for Hollywood star Norma Talmadge (1893–1957).

splendid colors, such a rich yet low diamonds that when introduced tastefully are extremely elegant. A natural sized chrysanthemum, for instance, made of purple and maroon-colored enameled gold, is of the Japanese variety having the thready, incurved petals. The disc of the flower is represented by a round, deep yellow diamond brilliantly cut. This is a brooch, and a design of Paulding Farnham.

By the 1893 Chicago World's Columbian Exposition, Kunz had assembled a collection of colored diamonds, set for the exposition in brooches and rings designed by Tiffany's star jewelry designer, Paulding Farnham. These included a 16.25-carat blue cushion cut, priced at $12,800; a 6.9-carat light salmon orange brilliant, at $5,800; an 11.53-carat cognac brilliant, paired in a brooch with a 4.375-carat brilliant of matching color, for $8,500; and two black, or "carbonado," brilliants from Bahia, Brazil, of 16.69 carats and 12.75 carats, at $16,500 and $4,000 respectively.

Jewelers' Review of August 17, 1893, described as follows the colorful Tiffany diamond display:

A collection of diamonds of both rare and unusual colors, many of them quite remarkable. The center one contains a rich plum-colored diamond suspended from a diamond bow-knot and surrounded by a wreath of

white brilliants. Directly beneath it is a smoky black diamond surrounded by a lily of the valley wreath of white diamonds. On one side is a blue white diamond suspended in the center of a floral wreath of brilliants, and directly opposite is a large brown diamond with a small brown one suspended from a chain of white brilliants. Beneath it, further down is a Renaissance brooch containing a beautiful salmon pink diamond.

Yellow diamonds from South Africa had become so plentiful, however, that Kunz decided to write off nearly 30 percent of the Tiffany II's cost, lowering it in the 1893 exposition registry ledger from $6,500 to $4,650. The Roman Girdle included twenty-one yellow brilliants ranging from the 77-carat Tiffany II and the next four largest stones of 34.78, 30.875, 29.655, and 23.94 carats, to the smallest stone of 9.19 carats—all told, just over 410 carats. It was priced at $25,000, or $61 per carat, retail, with Tiffany's traditional 33⅓ percent markup.

Kunz not only promoted colored diamonds at Tiffany & Co. but also succeeded in selling Tiffany collections of colored brilliants to other major jewelry houses. A multicolored diamond necklace was sold to the great Paris house of Bapst and exhibited at the 1889 Paris exposition. The Paris *Herald* of June 22, 1889, expressed "admiration for a necklet of large brilliants of all colors. This has no equal in the world, and is of inestimable value." Paulding Farnham, who certainly designed it with Kunz, noted that the "necklace was part of our stock from '84 to '86 . . . Sold to Bapst and spoken for by Mr. [Hamilton McKown] Twombly. . . . Price asked at exposition 800,000 francs ($160,000)."

Although Farnham may have exaggerated the price of the Twombly colored necklace, evidence indicates that Tiffany & Co. and Kunz certainly played a leading role in popularizing colored diamonds, even if the prices for colored brilliants remained quite low in comparison to the finest pure white stones.

In the 1880s and well into the 1890s, Kunz was still obtaining yellow diamonds for the same forty dollars per carat that George McClure had paid for the first colored diamond recorded in Tiffany's registry books in 1853 (which was a yellow Brazilian, not a South African stone).

Other colors were considerably more costly. Of the stones shown in Chicago in 1893, the rare 16.85-carat black carbonado diamond from Bahia, Brazil, was priced at around $875 per carat, while the 16.25-carat blue brilliant was priced at only $750 per carat, and the "salmon" stone at $625 per carat. Interestingly their retail prices were only 25 percent above cost, whereas pure white Indian stones were marked up the full 33⅓ percent above cost.

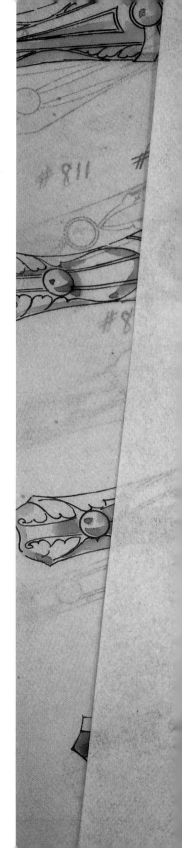

Ca. 1915 filigree bar brooches of diamonds set in platinum and gold placed upon archival drawings of bar brooches from the 1920s. The brooch at center has a 2-carat diamond, and the brooch at bottom has a 1-carat central stone flanked by two tiny butterflies.

The prices of Tiffany & Co.'s finest white diamonds were, at the time, about twice those of their finest colored stones. The most expensive pure white Golconda diamond sold by the firm prior to 1889 was the 26.14-carat antique cushion-cut "Rajah" diamond sold to famed Boston art collector Isabella Stewart Gardner, "Mrs. Jack," on April 1, 1886, for $35,100, or about $1,350 per carat. The perfect 25.18-carat brilliant in the pendant of the Hazelnut necklace shown in Paris in 1889 was priced at $45,000, or about $1,800 per carat.

Charles Lewis Tiffany successfully retained his position as King of Diamonds with the all-important help of George Frederick Kunz. Kunz, as noted, became Tiffany's chief gemologist in 1879 at the age of twenty-three. By 1883 he was also made a special agent for the U.S. Geological Survey and, in 1895, a special agent for the Department of Mines and Mining. He wrote extensively on diamonds and other precious stones, and he assembled the collection that forms the nucleus of the gemstone exhibit at New York's American Museum of Natural History, exhibiting it in the Tiffany display at the Paris Exposition of 1889. He also assembled the core of Chicago's Field Museum of Natural History's hall of gems for the Tiffany display at Chicago's World's Columbian Exposition of 1893. When pink spodumene was discovered near San Diego in 1903, it was named *kunzite* in his honor; then when pink beryl was discovered in Madagascar in 1911, Kunz named it *morganite* in honor of J. P. Morgan, the donor of the Hall of Gems at New York's American Museum of Natural History. Kunz also discovered a very rare milky bluish and highly phosphorescent type of diamond, which he named *Tiffanyite*. His fascination, which verged on obsession, with American gemstones led to the publication of his *Gems and Precious Stones of North America* in 1890.

One of George Frederick Kunz's dreams was to see the discovery of significant diamond deposits that he intuitively felt must lie somewhere on the North American continent. The discovery of the Dewey Diamond in 1855 in Virginia, he knew, could not be an isolated and unique occurrence. However, by 1950 only five diamonds of more than 20 carats had been found in North America.

Weight in Carats	Where Found	Date Found
40.23	Murfreesboro, Arkansas	1924
34.46	Peterstown, West Virginia	1928
27.21	Searcy, Arkansas	1925 or 1926
23.75	Manchester, Virginia	1855
20.25	Murfreesboro, Arkansas	1921

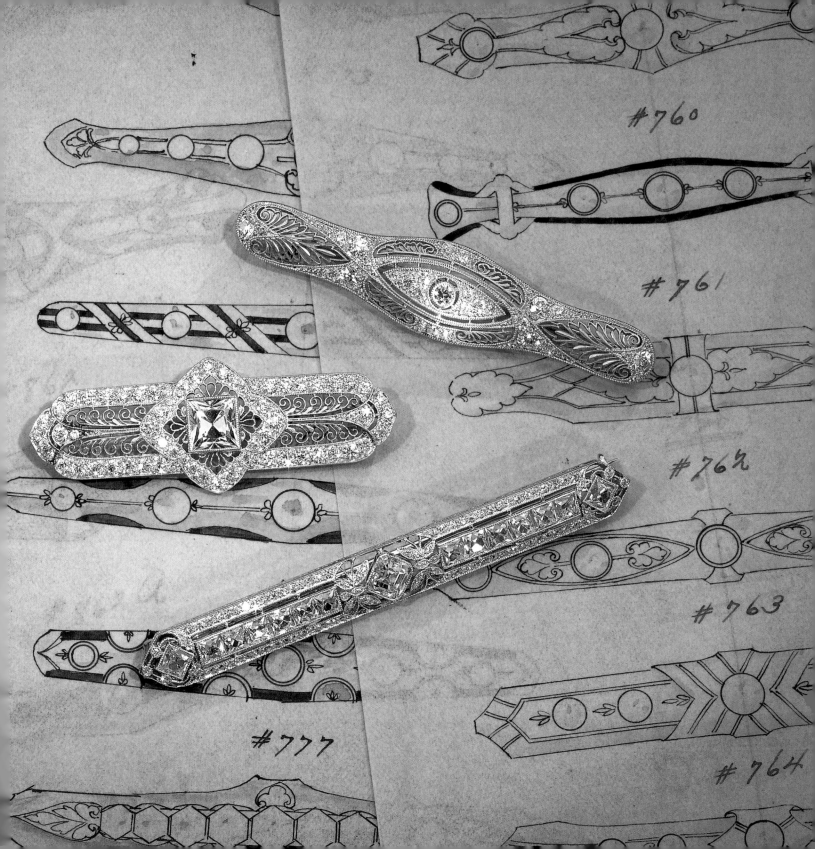

#760

#761

#762

#763

#777

#764

Two of the five had been found in Murfreesboro in Pike County, Arkansas, in the 1920s and the third Arkansas stone, although found approximately 140 miles from Pike County, must have originated in the same deposits, which were first discovered in 1906 by John Wesley Huddleston, who was searching for gold.

The New York daily newspaper, the *Sun*, on November 25, 1907, published a short article titled "Real Diamonds in Arkansas" explaining that a lesser diamond expert, Professor Philip Schneider of Syracuse University, who was investigating the Pike County diamond fields, reported that:

Much of the land inspected is worthless, but that a few acres, comprising what is known as the Huddleston and Money places, comprise the promising diamond land.

He says surface indications in this territory equal those in the Kimberley fields in South Africa. The earth resembles in every respect the soil in and around the Kimberley tracts.

Professor Schneider says there can be no doubt that genuine diamonds have been taken from the Huddleston tract.

Kunz was in Pike County investigating the diamond fields at the same time and gave his report to the Chicago *Record-Herald* five days later:

George F. Kunz, of Tiffany's, who is the highest authority on precious stones in this country and perhaps in any other country, has just returned from a visit to Murfreesboro, Pike County, Ark., to examine the spot where some diamonds were found not long ago. He says they are the real thing, and that the geological conditions are almost precisely those which occur in the neighborhood of the Kimberley diamond mines, South Africa.

"This is the first time diamonds have ever been found in their natural matrix on the American continent, and I consider it very important," said Mr. Kunz. "The soil and surroundings are similar to those in South Africa. The spot where they were found is beyond question the crater of an extinct volcano, and is filled with blue earth similar to that of Kimberley. It will take further investigation to show whether there are enough diamonds to make it pay to work the deposit, and whether the cost of working will permit of a profit. These questions can be decided within a few months, and if they can be decided in the affirmative, it is one of the best things I have ever struck. While most of the diamonds have been picked up on the surface of the igneous area, a few have been found among concentrates derived from washing the decomposed peridotite which much resembles that of Kimberley, and at least one diamond was found embedded in the decomposed peridotite itself. The evidence seems conclusive that the crystals are derived from the peridotite, and if so, this is the first occurrence of diamonds in place on either the North or South American continent."

Diamonds have been found loose in glacial deposits in about thirty places in Michigan, Wisconsin, Indiana, Ohio, and other states, but never before in natural conditions. This diamond discovery in Arkansas was originally made by a farmer named John Huddleston. Because the ground was green, he thought there might be copper under it and while prospecting around found one crystal and later two others. Since then fifteen or twenty of the natives have picked up diamonds.

Rough diamond weighing 27.21 carats found ca. 1925 by Mrs. Pellie Howell, when she was a ten-year-old girl helping her father chop cotton in Searcy, Arkansas. In 1946 Mrs. Howell sent the diamond to Tiffany's for authentication, and the company bought it for $8,500; it is believed to be the third-largest diamond found in the United States.

On January 9, 1907, in fact, Kunz, and Tiffany & Co.'s principal shareholders and officers Louis Comfort Tiffany, Charles Thomas Cook, and John Chandler Moore (later that year the third president of Tiffany & Co.) signed an agreement giving Kunz 25 percent and Tiffany, Cook, and Moore 75 percent of any interest he could acquire in the Arkansas diamond fields, up to a sum of $10,000.

Little came of this venture, as Arkansas diamond production was small; and the occurrence of diamonds was isolated and did not resemble a mineral vein or lode. By February 28, 1910, Kunz offered his conclusion on the phenomenon in New York's *World*: "Dr. Kunz of Tiffany's, who has examined property, says it gives great promise—gem producing area is small, an isolated freak of nature and has been all bought up, so he warns against a mining camp stampede."

Only three stones from Pike County are recorded to have been cut at Tiffany & Co. In the rough they weighed only 4.8 carats; cut they weighed a mere 2 carats.

On June 9, 1907, around six months before Professor Schneider's and Dr. Kunz's first published assessments of the Arkansas diamond discovery, the *World* printed a curious and, as it turned out, prophetic article:

TIFFANY'S SEEKING FOR GEMS IN CANADA

Canada has already demonstrated in some measure, the vast resources of her mineral wealth in many of the fields of mineral production so far discovered and exploited. It is predicted also, that at not far-distant day the world's latest and most marvelous diamond field will be discovered in Canada, and located, moreover, not so very far north of the capital itself.

Dr. H. M. Ami, a prominent member of the geological survey of Canada, gives it as his emphatic conviction that a diamond field— probably the richest in the world—will be found and developed in the great north land as soon as railway communication has been established to the Hudson Bay and vicinity. At different points important finds have recently been made by prospecting parties, and the fact that vari-colored natural carbon gems—white, yellow, and black—have been found scattered over a wide area, is held to indicate that they have been carried along by glacial drifts from some point further north.

The Tiffany's of New York, and other houses of the United States have sent representatives over the region in which diamonds have been found in Canada, and the favorable reports they have submitted, Dr. Ami states, are regarded as conclusive.

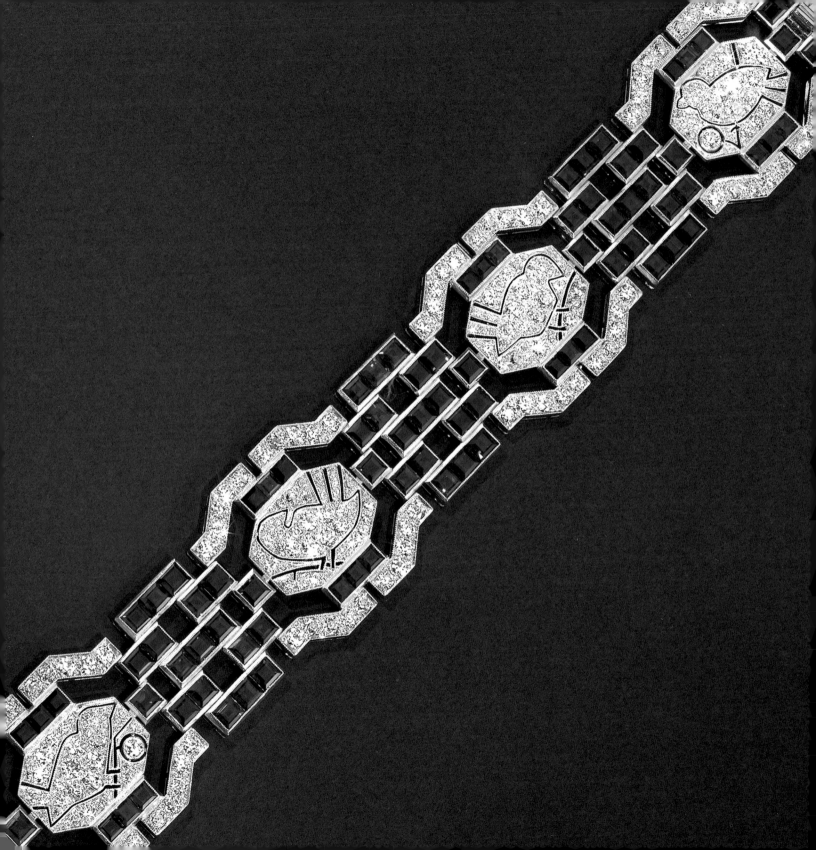

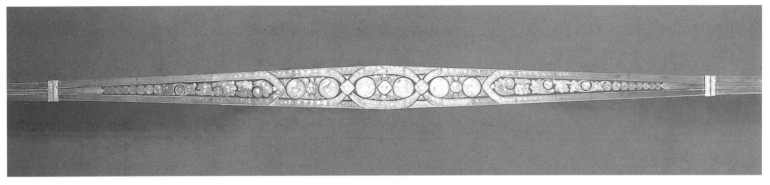

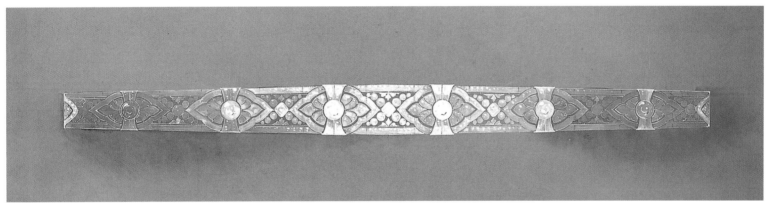

Kunz, however, would not live to see the discovery of the great present-day diamond fields of northwestern Canada, which were possibly at the origin of the stones deposited by glaciers in other parts of Canada and the northern United States, and which would play such a significant role in the story of Tiffany diamonds today. He would, however, see the popularity of diamond jewelry grow to even greater heights after the World War I, and after the definition in 1919 by the Belgium mathematician Marcel Tolkowsky of the "ideal" cut— which finally brought maximum brilliance to diamonds.

The near-ideal "American cut" so successfully promoted by Kunz and Tiffany & Co. from the 1880s until the 1920s had brought great success, distinction, and prestige to Tiffany & Co., as the preeminent purveyor of diamond jewelry to America.

By the 1893 Chicago World's Columbian Exposition, Tiffany & Co. was proud to have its own display of diamond cutting in the Mines and Mining Building "in connection with the DeBeers Diamond Mining Exhibit in the Cape Colony Section"—as the catalog stated. The company could also justly boast

OPPOSITE
Ca. 1930 platinum bracelet with sapphire links and diamond-pavé medallions with outlines of tiny birds.

ABOVE
Ca. 1925 drawings for diamond bracelets.

OVERLEAF
Important platinum-and-diamond bracelet, ca. 1925.

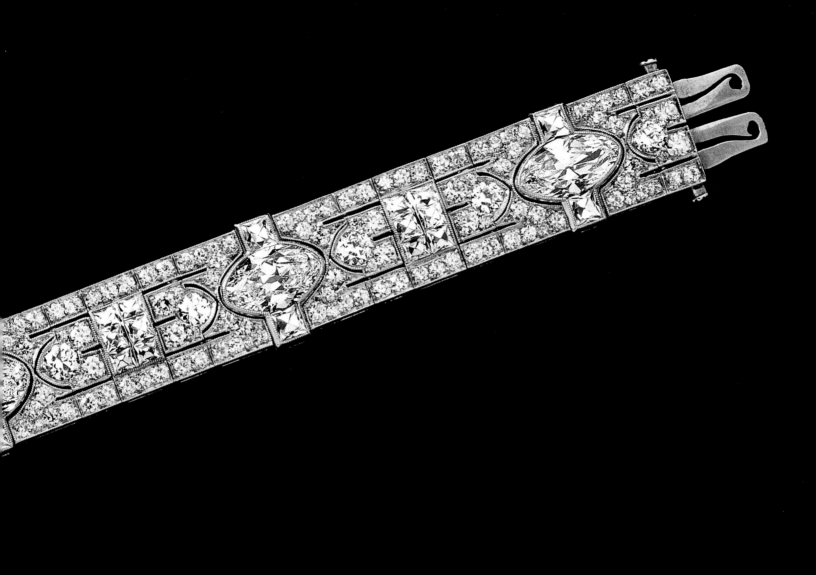

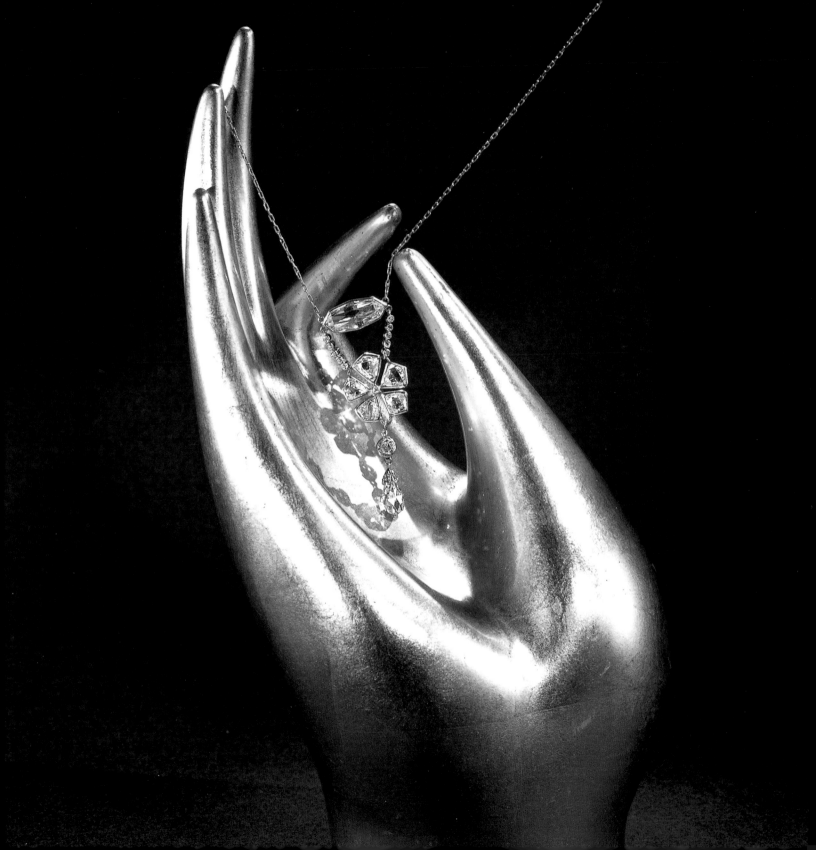

that, "In the Tiffany Pavilion there is exhibited a necklace of forty-two graduated brilliant cut diamonds, weighing 172.25 carats, which were cut directly from the rough by Messrs. Tiffany & Co. in the diamond-cutting works of their New York establishment, where they cut rough diamonds, recut broken or chipped diamonds, cut out imperfections, and recut poorly cut stones."

After the 1893 Chicago gold medals, the superiority of Tiffany diamonds was reconfirmed by the grand prize for jewelry at the Paris Exposition of 1900; by the highest award for jewels and jewelry at the Buffalo, New York, Pan-American Exposition of 1901; by the grand prize for gems and precious stones at the St. Louis Louisiana Purchase Exposition of 1904; and by the grand prize for gems and precious stones at the San Francisco Panama-Pacific Exposition of 1915.

If Tiffany diamonds dazzled the world at all the great world's fairs from 1889 to 1915, they would become even more dazzling with the ameliorations in diamond cutting that followed Tolkowsky's formulation of the "ideal" cut in 1919.

The decade that followed, known as the Roaring Twenties, the Cocktail Age, or the Art Deco period, was the platinum age of diamonds. No period has seen such a frenzy for diamonds. Colored gemstones were all but banished from fashionable jewelry wardrobes unless, of course, they were very large and set off by diamonds. The platinum blonde look of Hollywood's film goddesses of the 1920s, such as Marlene Dietrich, Jean Harlow, and Carole Lombard, was emulated everywhere, and the platinum blonde look demanded diamonds—and lots of them—set in platinum. Tiffany & Co., with George Frederick Kunz at the helm of its diamond business, was there to meet the demand, as it still is today, continuing on the course of committed excellence in gemology set by Dr. Kunz during his fifty-four-year tenure (1879–1933) as Tiffany's chief gemologist.

Kunz's cherished conviction that important diamond deposits—"The world's latest and most marvelous diamond field" as the *World* put it in 1907—would eventually be discovered in North America and very possibly in Canada finally turned out to be correct in 1991 when naturally occurring diamonds were discovered about three hundred kilometers northeast of Yellowknife, at Diavik in Canada's Northwest Territories. It happened eighty-four years after Tiffany & Co. and Kunz had first expressed their interest in Canada as a significant source of diamonds.

In 1999 Tiffany & Co. purchased a major interest in the Diavik enterprise and agreed to buy $50 million a year worth of diamonds from the mine.

On September 30, 2002, *Canadian Business* reported that: "Tiffany & Co.,

Diamond-and-platinum
bracelet and clip from
the early 1920s.

the world's most recognized jeweler, is setting up shop in the North—a true sign that the diamond industry has found a new love in Canada."

And the September 2003 issue of *Jeweler's Circular Keystone* added, "Tiffany is the world's first—and so far, only—retailer-turned-miner." Tiffany's new diamond-cutting and polishing facility opened in Yellowknife the next month. The Diavik mine yielded over 1.2 million carats of diamonds in 2003, of which Tiffany & Co. used nearly 100,000 carats, a marked increase over the 4.8 carats of rough in Tiffany's first delivery from Pike County, Arkansas.

The *Robb Report* of November 2003 observed under the heading "The American Way": "John Loring, Tiffany's renowned design director and historian, is particularly proud that Tiffany is selling diamonds sourced in North America."

Louis Comfort Tiffany, Tiffany's first design director and the greatest decorative artist America has produced, built a lavish eighty-room summer palace in 1902 at Cold Spring Harbor, on the north shore of New York's Long Island, naming it Laurelton Hall. He called its uniquely American Art Nouveau style "Grand Canyon Style" because the house, like the great canyon of the Colorado River, glowed with light and color.

"Fittingly," the *Robb Report* continued: "Tiffany named its cutting subsidiary in Yellowknife Laurelton Diamond Inc. Housed in a gray industrial compound in the frigid Northwest Territories, it is a far cry from the opulence of Laurelton Hall, but it represents the pioneering spirit of Louis Comfort Tiffany. It is a symbol of homegrown luxury and of Tiffany's steadfast independence from European tradition."

On October 26, 2004, Tiffany & Co. announced the signing of an agreement with Canada's Tahera Diamond Corporation to buy or market all diamonds from its Jericho mine, a newly discovered diamond deposit at Nunavut, Canada, 260 miles northeast of Yellowknife. The new agreement reinforced Tiffany's dedication to sourcing diamonds from known mines of origin sources, in a socially and environmentally responsible fashion, and to manufacturing those diamonds privately.

George Frederick Kunz was not party to the discovery of the rich diamond deposits of Canada's Northwest, but he did preside over Tiffany diamonds during both the Edwardian and the Art Deco periods—glittering periods in the history of jewelry. Fashionable women of the Edwardian period, at the outset of the twentieth century, followed the lead of England's statuesque and stylish Queen Alexandra with her fondness for diamond chokers, tiaras, and hair ornaments offset with ropes of pearls. Paulding Farnham designed lavish Edwardian diamond and pearl jewels for Tiffany & Co. in the first years of the Edwardian period.

Ca. 1936 necklace of sixteen marquise-cut diamonds (weighing a total of about 35 carats) and square-cut emerald "spacers," from the collection of Mrs. John Hay Whitney (1909–1998). One of the three strikingly beautiful Cushing sisters, Betsey Whitney was first married to President Franklin D. Roosevelt's son James Roosevelt, and occasionally served as hostess at the White House in the late 1930s. In 1941 she married Jock Whitney, the famous polo player, diplomat, venture capitalist, art collector, and publisher.

Floral tiara design for the
1939–40 World's Fair in
New York.

OPPOSITE AND
OVERLEAF
Drawings for all-diamond
tiaras for the 1939–40
New York World's Fair.

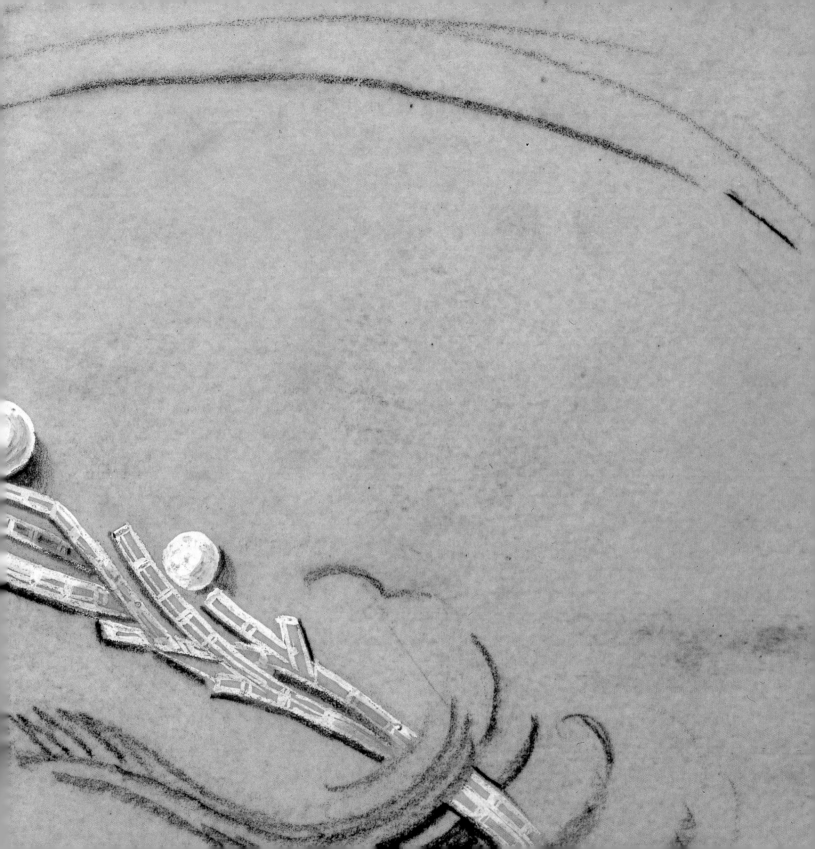

April 1939

OOPPOSITE

Drawing for one of Tiffany's major showpieces at the 1939–40 New York World's Fair— a necklace of 429 diamonds centered by a 200-carat emerald-cut aquamarine. The finished necklace, priced at $28,000, can be seen at bottom center of the photograph on page 161.

LEFT

Diamond brooch designs from 1939.

Left: Archival photograph of the diamond-and-ruby orchid brooch shown at the 1939–40 New York World's Fair. The brooch was set with 77 baguette diamonds weighing a total of 16.90 carats, and 392 additional diamonds weighing a total of 34.09 carats. The throat of the flower and the ribs of the petals were set with 49 rubies weighing 12.40 carats. The brooch was priced at $13,500.

Center: Archival photograph of a diamond bracelet of stylized flowers shown at the 1939–40 New York World's Fair. The 606 pear-shaped, marquise, baguette, and round diamonds weighed a total of 74.85 carats. The bracelet was priced at $26,000.

Right: Archival photograph of a diamond bracelet shown at the 1939–40 New York World's Fair. The 5 Extra River diamonds in the spray at center weighed a total of 28.82 carats; the other 277 diamonds weighed 40.30 carats. It was priced at $65,000.

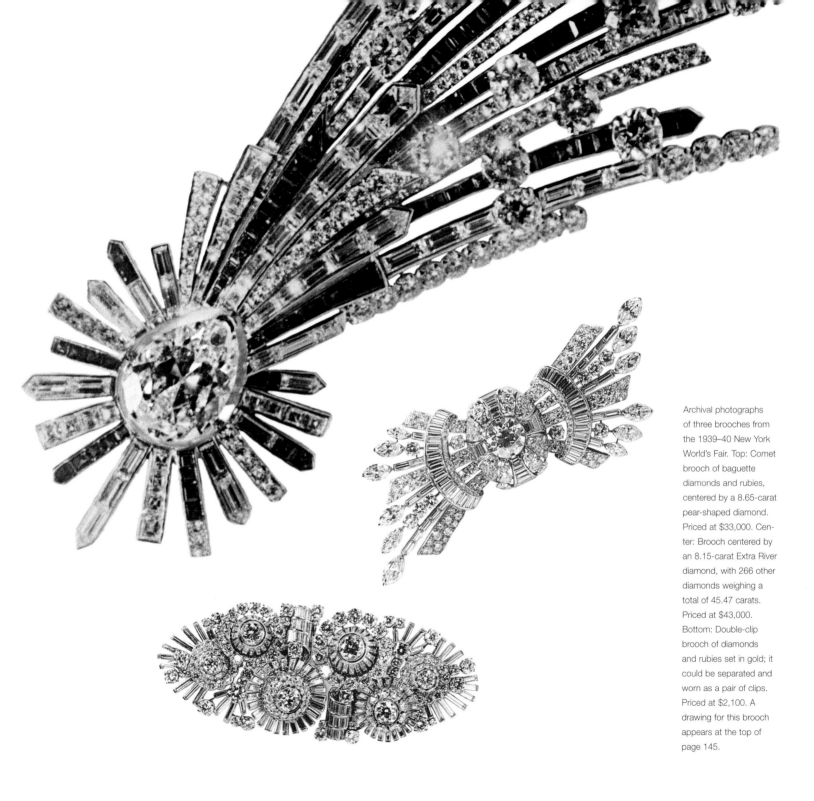

Archival photographs of three brooches from the 1939–40 New York World's Fair. Top: Comet brooch of baguette diamonds and rubies, centered by a 8.65-carat pear-shaped diamond. Priced at $33,000. Center: Brooch centered by an 8.15-carat Extra River diamond, with 266 other diamonds weighing a total of 45.47 carats. Priced at $43,000. Bottom: Double-clip brooch of diamonds and rubies set in gold; it could be separated and worn as a pair of clips. Priced at $2,100. A drawing for this brooch appears at the top of page 145.

In the Art Deco 1920s, fashion followed Hollywood, whose stars—all filmed in black and white—blazed with diamonds. As the stylish followed the lead of film, Tiffany's dazzling Art Deco jewelry consisted of diamonds, diamonds, and more diamonds—sometimes combined with rock crystals or pearls and the occasional black onyx accent—all in the highly stylized, angular, geometric deco designs that brought emerald-cut, square-cut, and baguette diamonds into the prominence at Tiffany's that they still enjoy today.

The advent of fashion photography in 1927 gave diamonds a run of unchallenged supremacy before the 1932 arrival of color film began to make representation of colored gemstones a possibility—even then, it would be years before the quality of color reproduction could make colored stones attractive enough for marketing to the general public. At *Vogue*, *Harper's Bazaar*, and *Town & Country* in the years following 1927, it was the norm to photograph fashion models accessorized (often to excess) with stacks of Art Deco diamond bracelets complimented by diamond earrings, and necklaces dripping with pear-shaped drops. Tiffany & Co., however, would refuse to loan its Art Deco jewels to fashion photo shoots until 1933.

Guided by George Frederick Kunz's exacting and unwavering demands for perfectly cut stones of the highest quality, Tiffany & Co. made superbly elegant Art Deco diamond jewels whose superiority of design and setting cause them to be fought for by today's connoisseurs of fine antique jewelry. However, Louis Comfort Tiffany, the internationally acclaimed god of Art Nouveau, retained control of Tiffany & Co. until his death in January 1933. Fashion photography was, of course, a phenomenon of the Art Deco movement—which contradicted everything Art Nouveau had stood for, so none of Tiffany's glorious Art Deco diamond jewels went before fashion photographers' cameras until 1933. Once there, they brought extraordinary glamour to the pages of *Vogue* in Edward Steichen's and Horst P. Horst's magnificent early fashion photographs—and to the pages of *Harper's Bazaar*—in the photographs of George Hoyningen-Huene, Man Ray, George Platt Lynes, and others.

All this culminated in 1939 in the visual pyrotechnics of Tiffany's diamond display in the House of Jewels at the great New York World's Fair—a burst of glory before the war years sent the jewelry industry into a prolonged lull.

During the 1950s and 1960s Tiffany & Co. rebuilt its diamond inventories into world-class collections of fine white diamonds of all cuts—round, emerald-cut, pear-shaped, and marquise—which Tiffany prides itself on to this day.

Then, with the 1974 introduction of "Diamonds-by-the-Yard," from Tiffany's great Italian-born jewelry designer Elsa Peretti, the doors of

Tiffany's jewelry exhibit at the 1939–40 New York World's Fair included what the company described as a "diamond spray and shell." The fireworks-like display, centered by the famous 128.54-carat Tiffany diamond, contained 634 other diamonds weighing a total of 234.13 carats. The Tiffany Diamond was then priced at $200,000.

Tiffany's diamond fashion jewelry collections opened to the young. Peretti single-handedly popularized smaller perfectly cut round diamonds with her solitaire-diamond neck chains and other Diamonds-by-the-Yard jewels, which included small-scale bezel-set stones irregularly stationed in fine 18-karat gold chains.

The Imperial Eighties, as that period of unparalleled prosperity was called, saw a revival at Tiffany & Co. of large-scale diamonds and a fondness for heart-shaped stones, huge emerald-cut stones, and starburst cuts. This renewed thirst for diamonds, brought on by the newly made fortunes of the 1980s, was eloquently immortalized by the leading photographer of jewels, Victor Skrebneski, with his memorable photographs of models ablaze with Tiffany diamonds in the opulent pages of *Town & Country*.

In 1999, after a 150-year adventure offering the finest available diamonds to the world of jewelry, Tiffany & Co. introduced a stunning new innovation: the now-celebrated Lucida cut. The culmination of many years of research and development, the Lucida diamond is one of the rare patented diamond cuts. The diamond's square mixed-cut shape, with wide corners, combines the classic elegance of a step-cut crown and a brilliant-cut pavilion. Together these two facet styles strike a balance between period cutting—with its emphasis on line— and modern-style cutting—with its emphasis on brilliance, dispersion of light, and scintillation.

Most recently, the Tiffany Legacy Collection again recaptures the perfection and romance of Tiffany diamonds. The Tiffany Legacy engagement ring is inspired by period jewels and features a lavish, diamond-encrusted setting with a patented cushion-cut center diamond.

From the round brilliant-cut diamond in the famous six-prong Tiffany Setting to the patented Lucida diamond and the recent Tiffany Legacy engagement ring, Tiffany diamonds are symbols not only of commitment, but also of trust, integrity, and craftsmanship—the hallmarks of Tiffany & Co. for more than eight generations.

John Loring

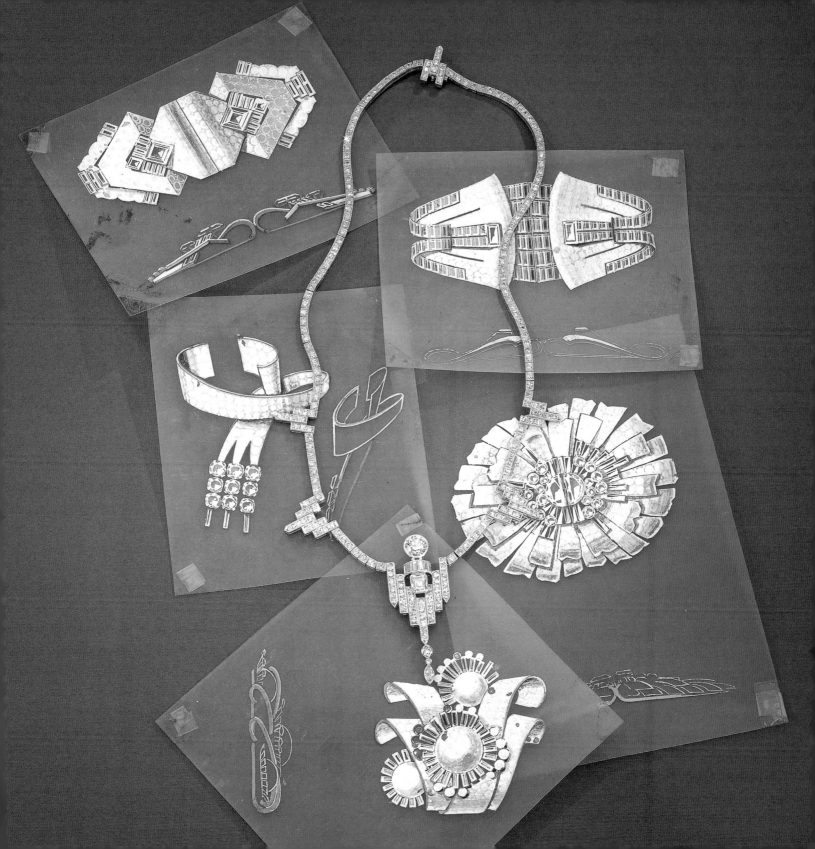

OPPOSITE

OPPOSITE
Señora de Barreda
de Chopita wearing
Suzanne Remy's velvet
hat shown with dia-
monds from Tiffany's.
Photographed by Horst
for *Vogue*'s August 15,
1941, issue.

LEFT
Drawings for diamond
brooches for the
1939–40 New York
World's Fair.

March 21st 1940

march 3/39

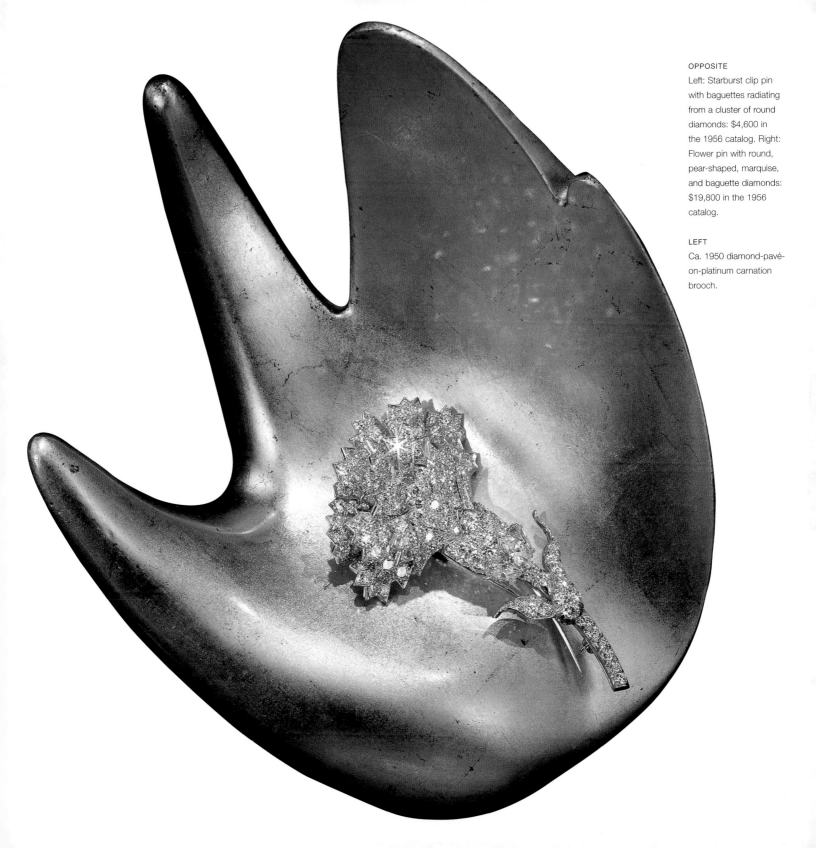

Double-strand
diamond necklace with
13 diamond pendants, 6
with marquise-shaped
drops. Priced at $17,400
in the 1951 catalog.

OPPOSITE
Necklace of round and
marquise diamonds set
in platinum, advertised at
$20,000 in the October
1957 issue of *Harper's
Bazaar*.

Fleurage necklace of 1,000 diamonds weighing a total of 44.59 carats, set in 18-karat gold and platinum, designed by Schlumberger in 1958 for Mrs. Paul ("Bunny") Mellon. She and her husband were among America's foremost philanthropists and art collectors.

OPPOSITE
Leaves and Flowers necklace of diamonds set in 18-karat gold, designed by Schlumberger ca. 1957 for Mrs. Nathaniel P. Hill, an heiress to the Campbell Soup fortune.

OPPOSITE

Rings of diamonds set in 18-karat gold and platinum designed by Jean Schlumberger. Left: Coronet ring with a 38.13-carat cushion-shaped canary diamond, 1970. Right: Trellis ring, 1956. Below: Six Bees ring with a 7.32-carat diamond, 1956.

LEFT

Two views of a diamond ring designed by Jean Schlumberger ca. 1968. The 70.98-carat yellow-brown diamond has a setting of crossed bands of round and baguette diamonds.

OPPOSITE
Frame clip featuring
a 44.35-carat cushion-
cut canary diamond,
designed by Schlum-
berger in 1958 and
made in 1969.

LEFT
Left: Seed Pod or
Conique bracelet of
white diamond-pavé and
114 yellow diamonds set
in 18-karat gold and
platinum, designed by
Schlumberger in 1966.
Above right: Three
Flowers diamond
bracelet designed by
Jean Schlumberger in
1960. The central
diamond weighs 3.06
carats.

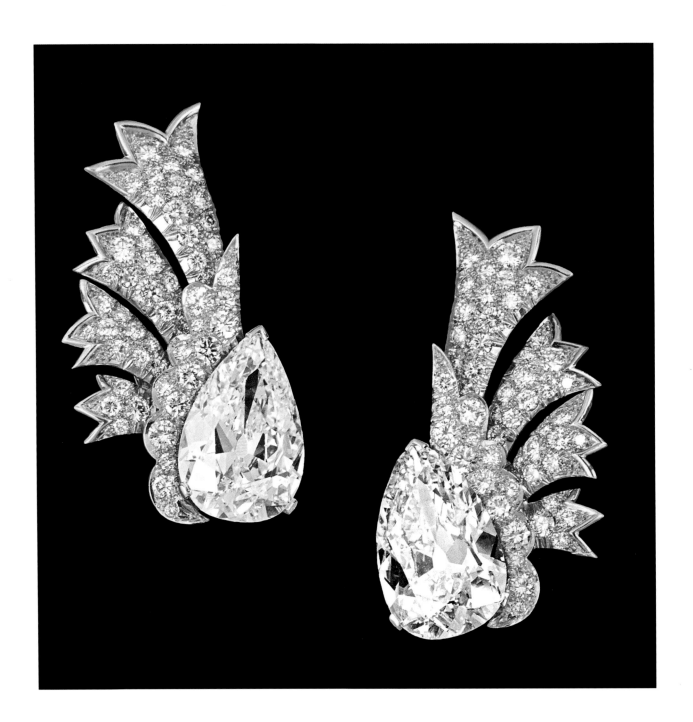

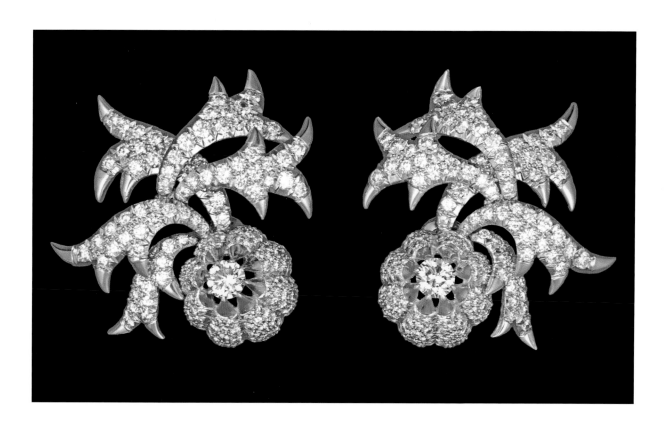

Two Leaves and Bud clip
designed by Schlum-
berger in 1958.

OPPOSITE
Schlumberger's Maple
Leaf clip of canary dia-
monds set in 18-karat
gold and white diamonds
set in platinum, originally
made for Bunny Mellon
in 1968.

Diamond-pavé-on-platinum jacket buttons. In its September 1963 issue *Harper's Bazaar* commented, "An extravagant echo of the Twenties, a superb stroke of chic in 1963, tailors' buttons turned into extraordinary jewels" (p. 253).

OPPOSITE
This Tiffany advertisement from the early 1960s featured a pear-shaped diamond engagement ring and a wishbone; the ad was designed by Tiffany's legendary master of window display, Gene Moore.

Sew it yourself kit... **TIFFANY & CO.**

NEW YORK
SAN FRANCISCO 233 POST STREET FIFTH AVENUE HOUSTON FIRST CITY NAT'L. BANK BLDG.

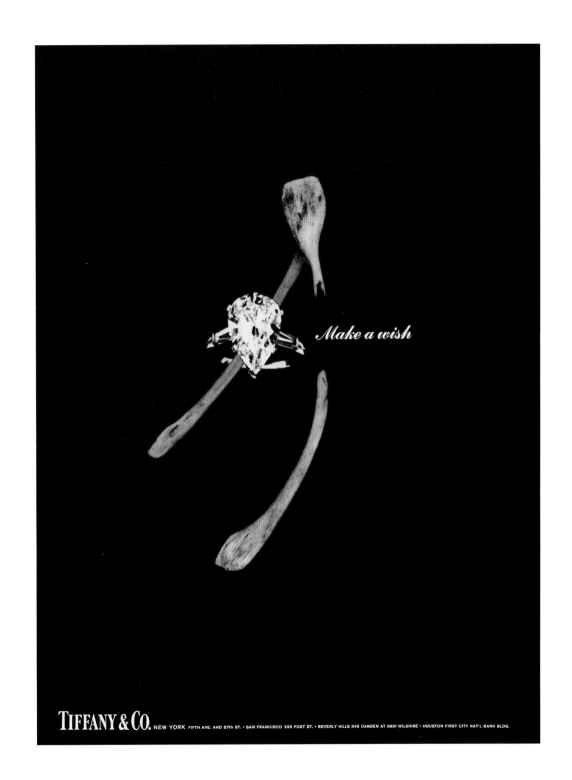

Make a wish

Tiffany diamond engage-
ment ring advertisement
from the early 1960s.

OPPOSITE
Tiffany Christmas advertisement from 1963 featuring
diamond-spray pins topped
by a diamond-star pin.

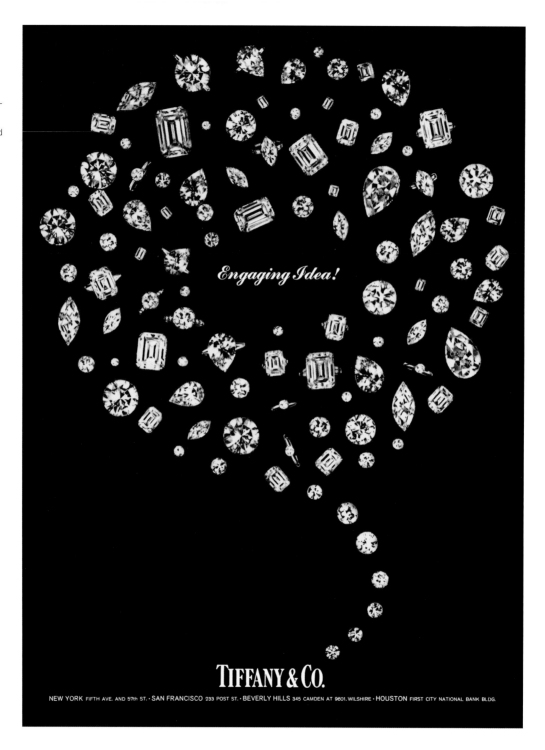

Engaging Idea!

TIFFANY & CO.

NEW YORK FIFTH AVE. AND 57th ST. · SAN FRANCISCO 233 POST ST. · BEVERLY HILLS 345 CAMDEN AT 9601, WILSHIRE · HOUSTON FIRST CITY NATIONAL BANK BLDG.

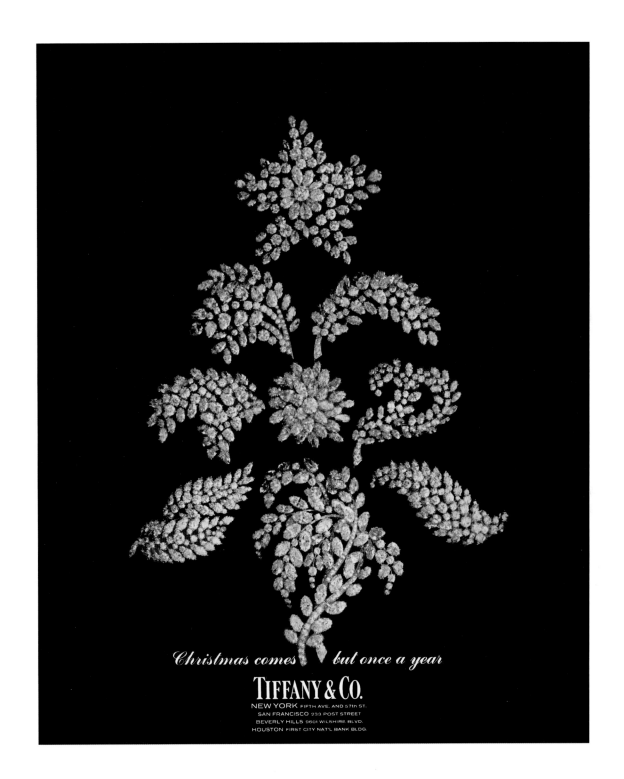

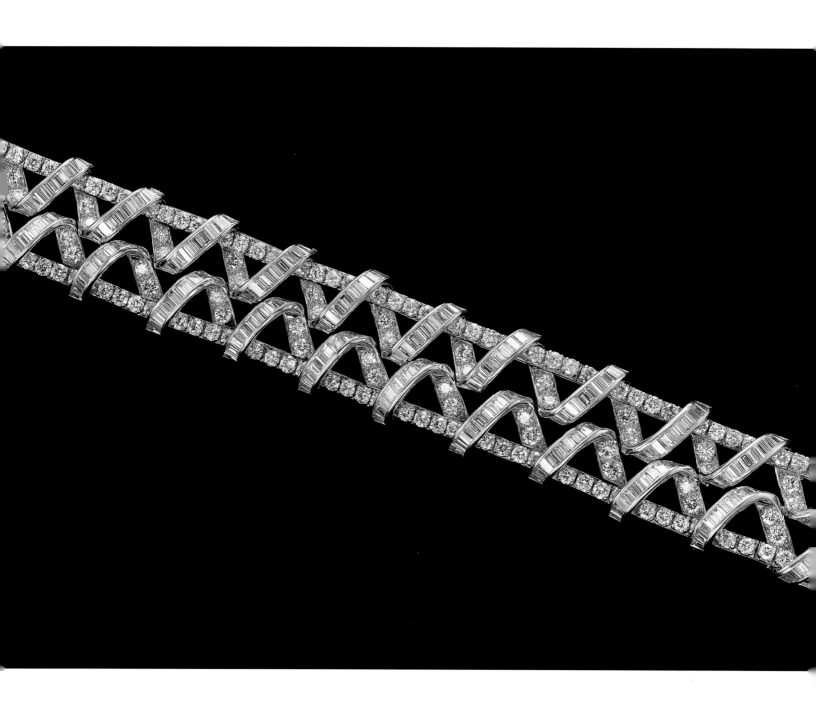

OPPOSITE
Bracelet of baguette and round diamonds weighing a total of about 40 carats set in platinum, designed by Schlumberger in 1956 and completed in 1957. Part of his first collection for Tiffany's, it was purchased by Paul Mellon (1908–1999) for his sister, Alisa Mellon Bruce.

LEFT
Brooch with sprays of diamonds set in platinum made in 1963, priced at $44,000. This brooch also appears at the bottom of the photograph on page 187.

Schlumberger's Sheaves
of Wheat clip with 81
yellow diamonds, 59
white diamonds, and a
central 7.58-carat blue
diamond. Purchased in
1964 by Babe Paley.

OPPOSITE
Schlumberger's 1960
Ribbons necklace of
diamonds and 18-karat
gold, here centered by
a Schlumberger clip set
with the 128.54-carat
Tiffany Diamond. Audrey
Hepburn wore this
necklace with this clip in
publicity photographs for
Breakfast at Tiffany's.

THIS PAGE
Left: Fruit clip of 56 diamonds set in 18-karat gold and platinum, designed by Schlumberger in 1955. Right: Schlumberger's Leaves necklace of 18-karat gold with pavé diamonds set in platinum. From the 1983 catalog.

OPPOSITE
Snowflake clip of 266 diamonds set in 18-karat gold and platinum, designed by Schlumberger in 1966.

OVERLEAF
René Bouché drawing of an elegant and eminently 1950s woman in an eminently 1950s sedan wearing a black dress and long white kid gloves; the drawing is overlaid with a 1990s Tiffany diamond necklace and matching earrings reminiscent of 1950s style.

Necklace of diamonds set in platinum, designed in 1979 by Angela Cummings, suggests rippling water. Cummings designed jewelry for Tiffany's from 1967 to 1984.

OPPOSITE
Seashell necklace of 18-karat gold and diamonds set in platinum, designed by Angela Cummings in 1979.

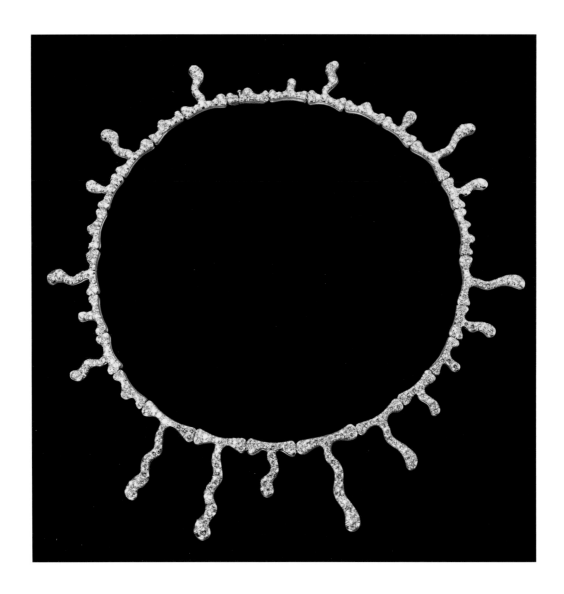

Star-shaped diamond-
and-platinum pendants
designed by Angela
Cummings in 1979.

THIS SPREAD AND OVERLEAF
Solitaire diamond rings set in platinum from the 1974 catalog; prices ranged from $190 to $322,000.

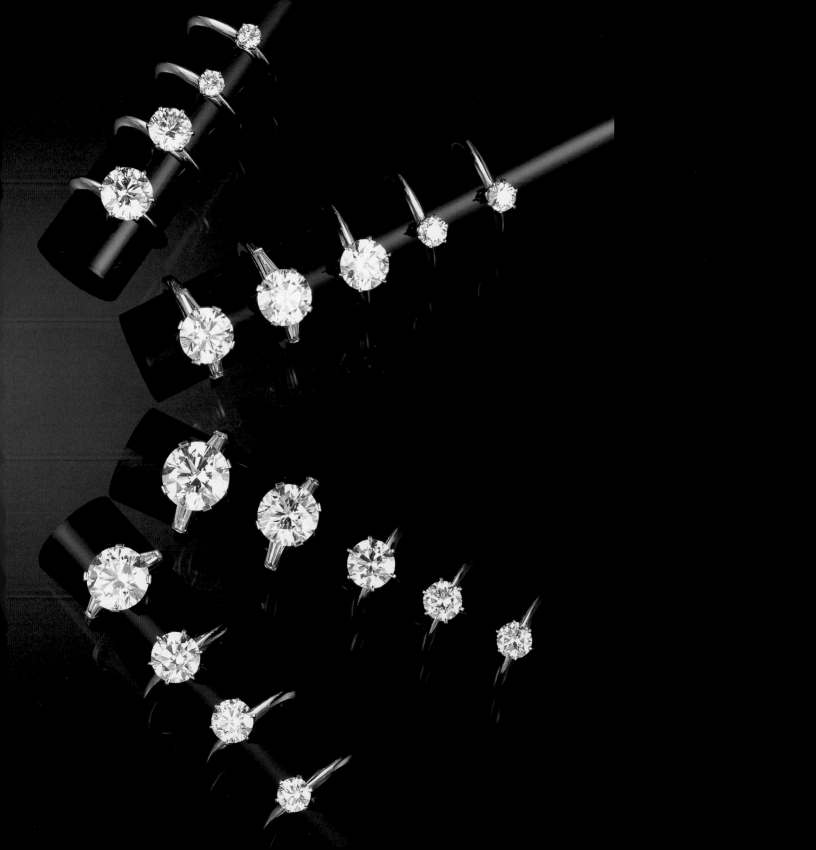

PREVIOUS SPREAD
One-of-a-kind gold-and-platinum rings set with colored diamonds, designed in 1983.

OPPOSITE
One of the most extravagant Tiffany diamond brooches of the twentieth century. The 107-carat canary diamond is surmounted by a 23-carat pear-shaped flawless diamond and surrounded by 80 carats of marquise and pear-shaped fine white diamonds. Designed by Maurice Galli and John Loring in 1988, it was priced at $15 million.

LEFT
Diamond-and-platinum jewelry from the 1983 Tiffany Classic Diamond Collection. Left: Cascade necklace of marquise, pear-shaped, and brilliant-cut diamonds. Below: Earrings of pear-shaped diamonds surrounded by rows of brilliant-cuts.

Garland necklace of
marquise, pear-shaped,
and round diamonds; the
matching earrings have
square diamond drops.
Below left: band ring
with 14 1-carat emerald-
cut diamonds. From the
1984 catalog.

OVERLEAF LEFT
Graduated brilliant-cut
diamond necklace set in
platinum. Left: Matching
double-diamond ring.
From the 1984 catalog.

OVERLEAF RIGHT
Solitaire diamond rings
set in platinum. Left
to right: Brilliant-cut,
emerald-cut, and
pear-shaped diamonds.
Designed in 1984.

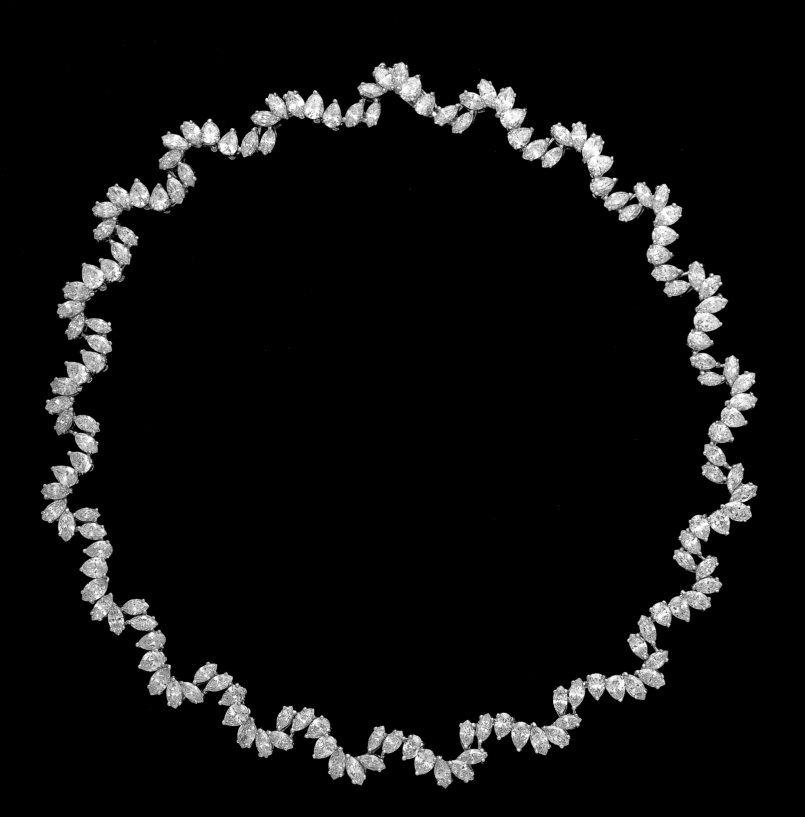

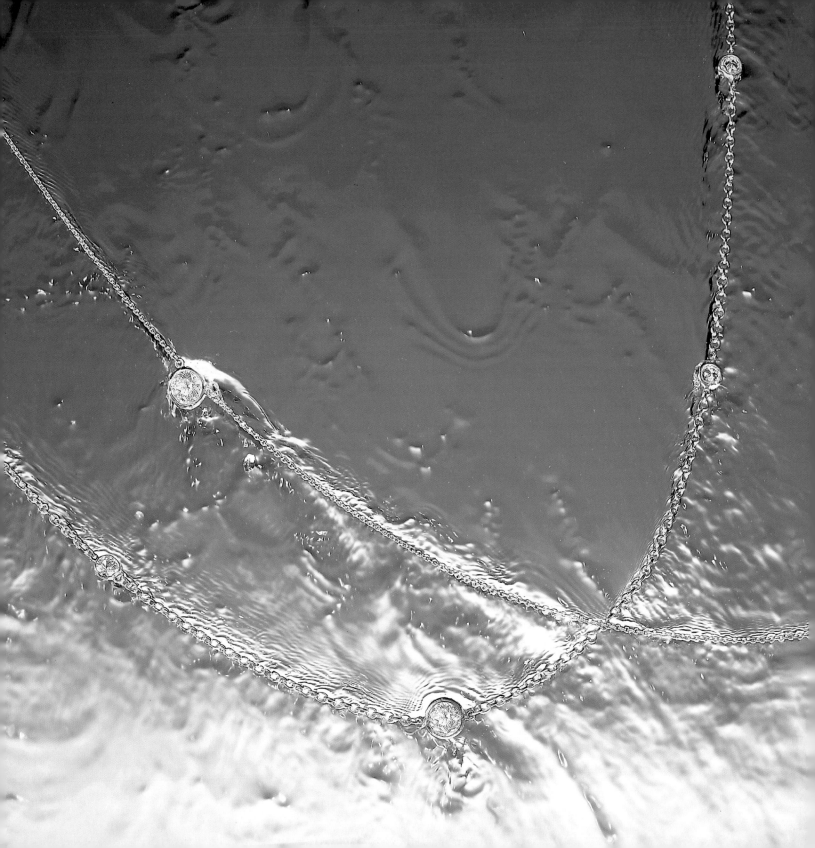

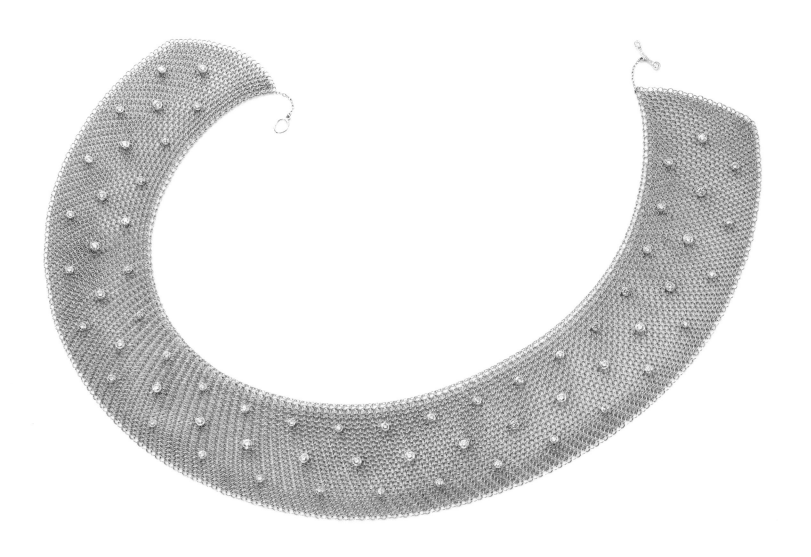

226

Raised Octagon ring of
diamonds set in 18-karat
white gold, designed
by Paloma Picasso.
The daughter of Pablo
Picasso and Françoise
Gilot, she designed her
first jewelry collection for
Tiffany & Co. in 1980.

OPPOSITE
Eighteen-karat gold
mesh bracelet with a
diamond-pavé clasp,
designed by Paloma
Picasso in 1981.

Original designs
© Paloma Picasso

228

Cooper bracelet of 468 diamonds set in 18-karat gold and platinum, designed by Schlumberger in 1958. The first bracelet was purchased by film star Gary Cooper (1901–1961).

OPPOSITE
Above: Schlumberger's Gazelle 18-karat gold clip with a diamond-pavé head, cabochon sapphire eyes, and diamond "leaves." Designed in 1963, the first Gazelle clip was purchased by investor and philanthropist Laurance S. Rockefeller (1910–2004).
Below: Seastar clip of diamond-pavé on platinum with 18-karat gold, designed by Schlumberger in 1957. It is set with 121 diamonds weighing a total of 6.57 carats. The first Seastar clip was purchased by venture capitalist and Vanderbilt heir William A. M. Burden (1906–1984).

Schlumberger's 1958
Flowers and Leaves
bracelet of diamonds
and 18-karat gold and
platinum representing
eight different flowers,
connected by leaves. It
contains 446 diamonds
weighing a total of 32.06
carats. Originally made
for Paul Mellon.

OPPOSITE
A floral garland necklace
of diamonds set in plat-
inum and 18-karat gold,
designed by Schlum-
berger. It is set with 214
diamonds weighing a
total of 35.81 carats.

OPPOSITE
The Atlas watch, designed in 1980 by John Loring and introduced in 1983, was named for the Atlas clock that has been on the front of Tiffany's New York stores since about 1853. Shown here is a version of the Atlas watch in platinum with a diamond bezel, along with a matching ring and bracelet from the Atlas jewelry collection.

LEFT
Elaborate Art Deco–inspired diamond necklace, designed in 2002. The pendant has baguettes around a marquise diamond, 6 marquise drops, and a central pear-shaped drop.

Art Deco–style diamond pendant with a pear-shaped drop from Tiffany's Jazz collection introduced in 2001. The pendant is part of a suite that includes a bracelet and earrings.

OPPOSITE
Art Deco–style diamond-on-platinum pendant with pear-shaped drops on a cultured–seed-pearl chain, designed in 2003.

The Tiffany Lace
diamond-on-platinum
collection, introduced in
2001. The collection's
starbursts were based
on the starbursts shown
on pages 36–37.

OPPOSITE
Tiffany Lace starburst
brooches.

LEFT
Tiffany Lace necklace
with starburst pendant.

Tiffany Lace bracelet of
miniature starbursts.

OPPOSITE
Tiffany Lace earrings and
necklace.

OPPOSITE AND BELOW
Tiffany Lace latticework
necklace and bracelet
based on a 1909 design
of miniature florets by
Louis Comfort Tiffany.

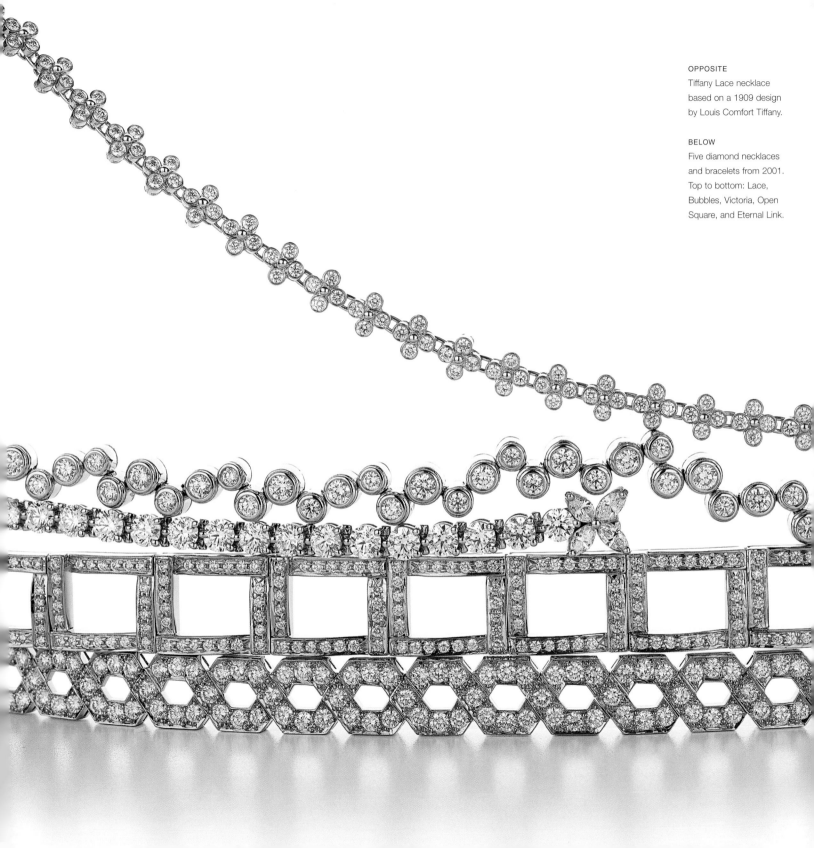

Garland diamond-on-platinum necklace and bracelet of flowering branches. The necklace is set with 126 marquise diamonds and 486 round diamonds together weighing a total of 49.70 carats; the bracelet, with 55 marquise diamonds and 199 round diamonds weighing a total of 22.97 carats.

OPPOSITE

Above: Pavé Pear
diamond bracelet, part
of a collection introduced
in 1999. Below: Tiffany
Legacy bracelet of dia-
monds set in platinum.

BELOW

Splash diamond bracelet
of 561 round diamonds,
weighing a total of 18.97
carats, set in platinum.

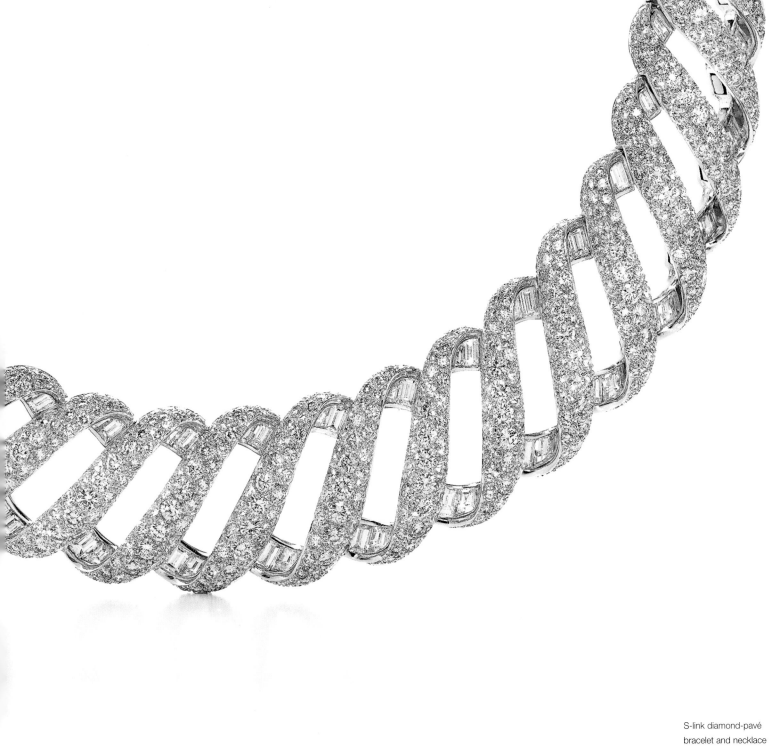

S-link diamond-pavé
bracelet and necklace
introduced in 1999.

Étoile diamond-pavé link
necklace introduced in
1998.

OPPOSITE
Tiffany Hearts diamond
pendants, introduced in
2003.

BELOW
Fireworks bangle
bracelet of diamonds set
in platinum.

RIGHT
Tiffany Bubbles necklace
of bezel-set diamonds.

OPPOSITE
Garland diamond neck-
lace and earclips, part
of a suite introduced in
1999, based on maiden-
hair-fern-motif designs
by Paulding Farnham for
the Buffalo Pan-Ameri-
can Exposition in 1901.

LEFT
Cluster necklace of diamonds set in platinum containing 166 round, pear-shaped, and marquise diamonds weighing a total of 40.50 carats. The pendant is centered by a 2.80-carat pear-shaped diamond.

OPPOSITE
Matching earrings.

Stunning necklace of 80 emerald-cut white and yellow diamonds set in platinum and 18-karat gold. Designed in 1999.

Diamond-and-platinum rings. Left to right: round white diamond flanked by pear-shaped diamonds, cushion-shaped pink diamond flanked by cushion-cut white diamonds, emerald-cut white diamond flanked by baguettes, cushion-shaped yellow diamond surrounded by white diamonds, pear-shaped white diamond flanked by baguettes.

OPPOSITE
Wreath diamond necklace based on Paulding Farnham's diamond-and-pearl maidenhair-fern-motif corsage ornament shown at the 1893 Chicago Exposition (see pages 98–99).

Chandelier earrings of bezel-set pear-shaped diamonds with briolette drops. From the 2003 catalog.

OPPOSITE

Platinum-and-diamond daisy brooch inspired by drawings in the Tiffany Archives. Introduced in 2003.

Four pairs of diamond-on-platinum earrings from recent collections. From left: Tiffany Jazz earrings, earrings with briolette drops, diamond-drop earrings, and three-drop Art Deco–revival earrings.

Pair of drop earrings,
each set with 2 pear-
shaped diamonds and
1 round diamond.

OPPOSITE
The classic six-prong
Tiffany Setting for
a solitaire diamond
engagement ring.

Tiffany Setting solitaire diamond engagement ring.

OPPOSITE
Above: The Lucida patented Tiffany diamond cut, introduced in 2001, is noted for its high step-cut crown, wide corners, and brilliant-style pavilion.
Below: Lucida diamond ring with a four-prong setting.

Fancy diamond rings augmented with baguette and channel-set white diamonds. Left to right: 6.72-carat cushion-shaped yellow diamond, 2.04-carat cushion-shaped "hot pink" diamond, 2.58-carat "mint green" emerald-cut diamond (high-quality green diamonds are extremely rare), 1.72-carat cushion-shaped orange diamond, and 2.45-carat "hydrangea" blue diamond.

Sumptuous ring with a fancy vivid yellow 3.22-carat oval diamond surrounded by white diamonds, flanked by pear-shaped white diamonds also surrounded by diamonds.

274

Left to right: Atlas white gold ring with two channel-set bands, Streamerica band ring studded with diamonds, 1937 ring with diamond baguettes, Étoile diamond-studded ring, Étoile diamond-pavé band ring, and Atlas ring with 3 channel-set diamonds.

BELOW

Extraordinary diamond
band rings from the
2001 catalog.

OPPOSITE

Diamond engagement
rings. Left to right: Étoile
diamond-pavé ring with
a central diamond,
Tiffany Setting solitaire,
emerald-cut diamond
ring with baguettes,
solitaire on a channel-set
band, Lucida solitaire
ring, 3-stone ring.

BELOW

Tiffany Legacy Collection
rings in platinum, with a
Lucida solitaire diamond
engagement ring.

OPPOSITE

Solitaire diamond on a
channel-set band of
diamonds in platinum.

FOLLOWING PAGES

Widely acknowledged as
a pioneer of multi-image
photography, Ryszard
Horowitz was born in
Kraków, Poland, in 1939.
In 1959, after finally
being allowed by Poland's
then-Communist
government to emigrate
to America, he enrolled
in New York's Pratt
Institute. There he was
awarded an apprentice-
ship to the legendary
Alexey Brodovitch, one
of the most influential
figures in the world of
editorial design and
photography. In 1967
he opened his own
studio in New York City,
and since then his
photographs have been
published and exhibited
around the world. The
following series of seven
photographs was
commissioned by Tiffany
& Co. and made in
New York City in 2004.
*Photographs © Ryszard
Horowitz 2004.*

PAGE 280

35.63-carat D color,
internally flawless
emerald-cut diamond.

PAGE 281

35.91-carat D color,
internally flawless pear-
shaped diamond.

PAGE 282

A very rare 1.59-carat
emerald-cut fancy
purplish-pink diamond.

PAGE 283

5.51-carat rectangular,
modified brilliant-cut
fancy vivid yellow
diamond.

PAGE 284

Another shot of the
35.63 D color, internally
flawless emerald-cut
diamond.

**PAGE 285 AND
ENDPAPERS**

11.61-carat D color,
internally flawless
brilliant-cut diamond.

PAGE 286

Gouldian finch with
13.97-carat D color,
internally flawless heart-
shaped diamond.

GLOSSARY

AIGRETTE. Featherlike hair or hat ornament

BAGUETTES. Long, narrow emerald-cut gemstones

BEZEL-SET. Gem set in a thin strip of metal to secure it in a mounting

BOX-SET. Gem set in a square mounting

BRILLIANT. Diamond proportioned and faceted to refract and reflect light.

BRILLIANT CUT. Cut with trangular and kite-shaped facets that radiate out from a central point. The modern brilliant cut (also called the American brilliant cut) was developed in Boston in the 1880s by Henry D. Morse and Charles M. Field and was soon adopted by Tiffany & Co. Its optical principles were confirmed in a 1919 treatise by Belgian mathematician Marcel Tolkowsky. The European brilliant cut, developed in 1940, is a variation of the American brilliant cut.

BRIOLETTE. Drop-shaped gemstone cut with small triangular facets.

CANARY. Strong yellow rarely found in diamonds. The famous Tiffany Diamond is a true canary, but yellow diamonds of less intense color are often called canaries.

CARAT. Unit of weight used for gemstones. The modern metric carat is 200 milligrams. It was standardized in 1911 partly due to the urging of Tiffany gemologist George Frederick Kunz.

CARBONADO. Rare black-gray diamonds from Bahia, Brazil

CLEAVING. Splitting a rough diamond along a plane parallel to one of its faces to remove impurities, flaws, or cracks

CORSAGE ORNAMENT. Jewel worn across the bodice—sometimes extending from shoulder to shoulder—in the late nineteenth century

CROWN. Upper part of a faceted gemstone

CULET. Point or facet on the base of a cut gemstone. A pointed culet is sometimes called a "closed culet."

CUSHION-SHAPED. Square or rectangular gemstone with rounded corners

DEMANTOIDS. Green garnets, usually from Russia's Ural Mountains

EMERALD-CUT. Cut with facets lined in concentric rows parallel to the girdle. Often used for rectangular or square gemstones.

FACET. Polished flat surface

FANCY. Term used for colored diamonds and unusual cuts

GOLCONDA. Diamonds of Indian origin

GIRDLE. Narrow band separating the crown and pavilion of a cut gemstone

KARAT. Measure of the fineness of gold. Pure gold is 24-karat. Most jewelry is 18-karat (75 percent pure); it is alloyed with copper, silver, or other metals for durability.

MARQUISE. Long, narrow oval with pointed ends

OLD EUROPEAN CUT. Term used for diamonds cut before the acceptance of the American brilliant cut

OLD MINE CUT. Cushion cut introduced in Brazil about 1730

PAMPILLES. Long pendants of gemstones (usually diamonds) of descending sizes that terminate in tapering, pointed gemstones

PARURE. Matching set of jewelry

PAVÉ. Small gemstones (usually diamonds) set closely together to form a continuous surface

PAVILION. Lower part of a faceted gemstone

PEAR-SHAPED. Teardrop

RIVER. Term formerly used for the clarity of diamonds; *see* Water.

RIVIÈRE. Necklace of brilliant-cut diamonds graduated in size

ROSE-CUT. Round with triangular facets in a dome shape over a flat base

SAUTOIR. Long chain necklace

TABLE. Largest facet on the top of a cut gemstone

WATER. Term formerly used for the clarity of diamonds. Terms such as "first water," "finest water," "extra river," "extra extra river" referred to colorless, flawless diamonds. Today the color and clarity of diamonds are often graded on a scale by the Gemological Institute of America (GIA).

A TIFFANY DIAMOND RING

THE GEMOLOGICAL STANDARDS FOR SUPERIOR BEAUTY

THE CELEBRATED TIFFANY SETTING,
THE RING WHOSE BEAUTY HAS
NEVER BEEN SURPASSED.

WHITE LIGHT

THE BEAUTY OF ANY DIAMOND
IS LARGELY DETERMINED BY
THE AMOUNT OF WHITE LIGHT
RETURNED TO THE EYE.
THE MISSION OF
EVERY TIFFANY DIAMOND IS TO
MAXIMIZE THAT BEAUTY.

THE GEMOLOGICAL STANDARDS IN THE
FOLLOWING PAGES REFER ONLY TO
ROUND-BRILLIANT DIAMONDS FROM
.18 TO 2.99 CARATS SET IN CERTAIN RING
STYLES. ROUND-BRILLIANT DIAMONDS
SMALLER OR LARGER, FANCY-SHAPED
DIAMONDS, AND FANCY-COLORED DIAMONDS
EACH HAVE THEIR OWN SPECIALLY
TAILORED STANDARDS OF EVALUATION.

TABLE OF CONTENTS

ONLY A DIAMOND

There are hundreds of recognized gemstones in the world today. Yet only one has all the virtues that make it worthy of an engagement ring, the enduring symbol of love and commitment. A diamond of superlative quality is a marvel to behold.

A diamond is brilliant. It returns more white light to the eye.

A diamond disperses fire. Acting as a prism, it efficiently gathers and refracts light into a spectrum of beautiful colors.

A diamond scintillates. It sparkles with reflected and refracted light which can be seen at a great distance.

A diamond endures. It is the hardest natural substance on earth.

A diamond is purer. It is the purest of all the gemstones. A diamond is virtually pure carbon formed millions of years ago into a crystal, many miles below the surface of the earth.

A Tiffany diamond is rare. One must cull through tons of ore to find a single gem-quality, 1-carat diamond. Yet only a very small fraction of those gem-quality stones ever meets Tiffany standards.

CHARLES LEWIS TIFFANY ON THE FLOOR OF
HIS UNION SQUARE STORE.

THE WADE FAMILY NECKLACE, CREATED BY
TIFFANY IN 1900. THIS SUMPTUOUS NECKLACE
IS LITERALLY DRIPPING IN DIAMONDS
OF EXTRAORDINARY SIZE AND QUALITY.

AT THE TIFFANY GEMOLOGICAL LABORATORY,
A TEAM OF HIGHLY TRAINED PROFESSIONALS
CAREFULLY EXAMINES DIAMONDS
USING BINOCULAR MICROSCOPES
THAT ALLOW UP TO 60X MAGNIFICATION.

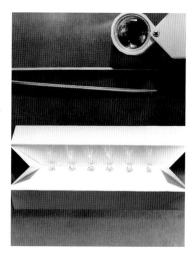

AMONG THE GEMOLOGIST'S TOOLS ARE
"MASTER DIAMONDS," WHICH ARE USED
TO AWARD A PRECISE COLOR GRADE
TO EACH TIFFANY DIAMOND.

TIFFANY'S DIAMOND HERITAGE

THE BEST THERE IS, FOR MORE THAN 150 YEARS

It was Tiffany & Co. that introduced the engagement ring as we know it today. The celebrated six-prong "Tiffany Setting" lifts the diamond above the band and into the light. The result is a ring whose brilliance has never been equaled.

In 1848 the New York City newspapers dubbed Charles Lewis Tiffany "The King of Diamonds." And with good reason. The quality of Tiffany diamonds was then, and remains, exemplary. In the spring of 1887, Tiffany shocked the world by purchasing the French crown jewels. From this time on, Tiffany became the world's authority on the finest diamonds.

Soon Tiffany designers were creating brilliance of their own. From the glittering 1890s on, timeless Tiffany designs graced women from the finest families: the Astors, the Vanderbilts, the Morgans. Celebrities from the theater, sports, and ultimately European royalty and Hollywood stars began to prize Tiffany diamond designs.

Around the world, museums treasure the Tiffany design aesthetic, from the Art Nouveau period to Art Deco to today's modern classics. Year in, year out, the passion for Tiffany diamonds is clearly demonstrated in the world's auction houses.

Today, the world-famous 128.54-carat Tiffany Diamond is on permanent display in the New York flagship store—proof positive of Tiffany's diamond legacy. But nowhere is a Tiffany diamond more beautiful or more treasured than in its place of honor, on the hand of a woman.

THE TIFFANY GEMOLOGICAL LABORATORY

A SEPARATE GRADING LABORATORY

For the protection of customers, Tiffany & Co. maintains a self-regulating diamond-grading facility located outside our flagship store. This state-of-the-art scientific laboratory is regularly certified by independent quality system auditors and is unparalleled in the retail business. Its job is to make certain that Tiffany diamonds meet Tiffany's exacting standards.

On staff at the Tiffany Gemological Laboratory is a professional team of expert diamond graders. Each holds a gemological diploma and has extensive grading experience. Every Tiffany grader is required to pass a rigorous Tiffany diamond instruction program prior to grading Tiffany stones.

Tiffany Graded Diamonds
Tiffany round-brilliant diamonds receive individual Tiffany grades for cut, color, clarity, and carat weight and are evaluated for presence. In the process, outside diamond reports are occasionally overruled. When a Tiffany gemologist sees a diamond that is on the borderline between two grades, the stone is automatically assigned the lower grade. Many stones are rejected and returned to the marketplace.

Diamonds that do meet the Tiffany quality parameters are awarded the Tiffany Diamond Certificate. There is no more trusted gemological certificate in the world.

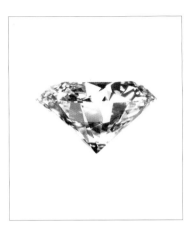

A TIFFANY DIAMOND IS MEASURED BY AT
LEAST 26 QUALITY PARAMETERS.

THESE ARE TIFFANY FACETS. NOTE THE
CLEAN, CRISP FACET JUNCTIONS
EMPHASIZING MATHEMATICAL PRECISION
FOR SUPERIOR INTERPLAY OF LIGHT.

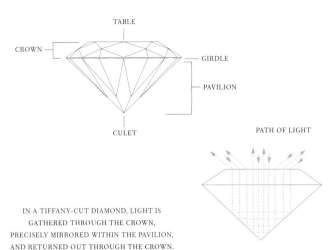

DIAMOND NOMENCLATURE

IN A TIFFANY-CUT DIAMOND, LIGHT IS
GATHERED THROUGH THE CROWN,
PRECISELY MIRRORED WITHIN THE PAVILION,
AND RETURNED OUT THROUGH THE CROWN.

PATH OF LIGHT

STRICTER STANDARDS, GREATER BEAUTY

MOVING BEYOND POPULAR TERMINOLOGY

THE COMMONLY REFERRED TO "4C'S"
ARE AN OVERSIMPLIFIED MEASURE
OF TRUE DIAMOND QUALITY.
TIFFANY HAS REFINED THESE
POPULAR DEFINITIONS AND
ITEMIZED SPECIFIC LOOPHOLES
AND DANGERS. TIFFANY HAS ALSO
INTRODUCED A SET OF KEY TIFFANY
DIAMOND QUALITY EVALUATIONS
COLLECTIVELY CALLED "PRESENCE."

CUT

CLARITY

COLOR

CARAT WEIGHT

PRESENCE

CUT

THE ULTIMATE SACRIFICE

Gemologists use the term "cut" when
referring to the facet proportions on the
surface of a diamond. More than any
other factor, the precise positioning of
these facets determines the beauty of
the stone. The Tiffany round-brilliant
diamond is properly proportioned and
cut to achieve the perfect balance of
brilliance, dispersion, and scintillation.
That is the secret of its superlative beauty.

But if a diamond cutter chooses to
maximize size instead of beauty, the stone
usually loses brilliance, dispersion, and
scintillation. True to our stricter standards,
Tiffany routinely sacrifices significantly
more of the rough diamond than is
customary in the industry. Beauty trumps
size every time.

The Physics of Beauty
The Tiffany round brilliant-cut stone
has 57 or 58 perfectly aligned facets that
work together in absolute geometric
unison.

The facets on the crown (top) function
as windows, collecting light into the heart
of the stone. The facets on the pavilion
(bottom) mirror the light back and forth
in a frenzy until it bursts out through the
crown in a fiery blaze.

All of the proportions in this stone
are critical and specifically prescribed by
Tiffany. There is a defined relationship
between the table, the crown, the pavilion,
and the girdle. The angle of every facet
is precisely fashioned and then measured
for accuracy.

A Word To The Wise
An inexperienced diamond cutter will
ruin a fine stone. An unscrupulous
diamond cutter will easily deceive the
uninformed buyer. What follows are
tricks found routinely in the marketplace,
but not at Tiffany & Co.

Beware Of Facet Claims
Tiffany's round brilliant-cut diamond has
57 or 58 facets, depending on the absence
or presence of a culet. This has been
demonstrated to be the most effective
number of facets to maximize light
return. Beware of claims that diamonds
with additional facets are superior.
Including many more facets does not
translate to more brilliance. Quite the
opposite!

Worthless Carat Weight
Because carat weight is always a factor
in pricing, some diamond cutters will
attempt to trick casual buyers. For
example, by creating an excessively thick

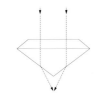

FISHEYE: PAVILION TOO SHALLOW

NAILHEAD: PAVILION TOO DEEP

IMPERFECTLY CUT STONES LEAK LIGHT,
SIGNIFICANTLY DIMINISHING BRILLIANCE.

girdle, carat weight (and price) is increased. Brilliance and beauty are, of course, noticeably impaired.

Fool the Eye
A diamond can be fashioned to create the illusion of a larger stone. It goes without saying that such stones exhibit diminished light behavior.

Fisheye
When a diamond is cut with a shallow pavilion and large table size, it produces a dull stone. And even worse, it creates an ugly "fisheye" effect when viewed through the crown.

Nailhead
When the pavilion of a diamond is too deep, a darkening "nailhead" effect appears in the middle of the stone.

CLARITY

A NEW DEFINITION
FOR A FUZZY TERM

A diamond's clarity rating is a key measurement and consideration. This rating has a direct effect on a diamond's price. And, of course, on the brilliance of the stone.

Virtually all diamonds have imperfections called inclusions and blemishes. A stone is said to be "flawless" if, under ten-power magnification, no internal flaws (clouds, feathers, pinpoints) and no external imperfections (scratches, pits, nicks) are visible. A truly flawless diamond is extremely rare and priced accordingly.

All gem-grade diamonds can receive a clarity rating based on an industry standard scale. As the chart (right) demonstrates, diamond clarity ratings range from FL (flawless) to I3 (heavily included).

FL
FLAWLESS

IF
INTERNALLY
FLAWLESS –
MINOR SURFACE
BLEMISHES

VVS1-VVS2
VERY, VERY
SLIGHTLY
INCLUDED

VS1-VS2
VERY
SLIGHTLY
INCLUDED

Tiffany will only sell diamonds of
VS2 or better.

SI1   SI2

SLIGHTLY INCLUDED

I1   I2   I3

IMPERFECT–EYE-VISIBLE INCLUSIONS

THE TIFFANY GEMOLOGICAL
LABORATORY REJECTS DIAMONDS
THAT FAIL TO MEET
TIFFANY STANDARDS.

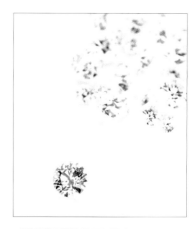

TIFFANY ROUND BRILLIANT-CUT DIAMONDS

Tiffany's Stricter Standards for Clarity
Tiffany, through its Tiffany Gemological Laboratory, sets and enforces diamond clarity standards that others so often ignore. In the process, other diamond reports may be overruled. A diamond with a borderline clarity rating automatically receives the lower rating.

– Inclusions visible to the naked eye are rejected.
– Of the eleven clarity grades, Tiffany accepts only the top six.
– Any enhancements or alterations to the diamond are totally unacceptable.
– Tiffany diamonds are thoroughly inspected before and after being set.
– Tiffany is unique in not awarding a "flawless" clarity grade to set stones. The reason: the setting obscures the grader's view of the diamond, making the award of a perfect grade questionable.

BLACK INCLUSION

LASER DRILL HOLE

CHIP

SURFACE INCLUSIONS

COLORLESS　　　NEAR COLORLESS

FAINT YELLOW　　　VERY LIGHT YELLOW

LIGHT YELLOW

A TIFFANY DIAMOND MUST BE
RATED COLOR "I" OR BETTER.

No Rude Surprises

As a matter of policy, Tiffany gemologists are always on alert for serious diamond imperfections. The informed buyer should know that other retailers may have very different standards, indeed.

Black Inclusions

Unfortunately, these distracting imperfections are very common. Tiffany customarily rejects black inclusions.

Chips

A chipped diamond is an inexcusable transgression and should be universally rejected. Unfortunately, surface chips are quite common, especially those carefully hidden under the prongs of a ring's setting. Tiffany does not accept chips.

Laser Drill Holes

In an attempt to market inferior diamonds, some will try to remove imperfections by drilling holes with a laser into the stone.

This flagrant violation of the stone's integrity can be cleverly disguised by injecting foreign material into the laser hole. Tiffany rejects laser-drilled diamonds, categorically.

Surface Inclusions

Inclusions that break the surface of the stone are a potential threat to the diamond and are rejected by Tiffany. These particular flaws create weakness that can result in a chipped or cracked stone.

Finding Hidden Flaws

The untrained eye may have difficulty identifying some clarity imperfections that are blatantly obvious to any gemologist. Tiffany systematically rejects the following common defects.

Pervasive Clouds

Milky clouds throughout the diamond crystal produce a dull stone. Buyers need to be aware of these unsightly inclusions.

Extra Facets

For a variety of reasons, some diamond cutters will add an extra facet or two or three. Sometimes these are included to remove or hide a defect. Sometimes it is simply poor workmanship. Beware of extra facets.

Significant Graining

Fine graining is a natural part of the crystal growth process and is found in most diamonds, including the very best. Significant graining, however, is an unfortunate and frequent flaw found both on the surface and within the stone. It is characterized by lines, streaks, or waves. Any diamond with significant surface or internal graining is automatically rejected by Tiffany.

Knots

Within a diamond crystal it is not unusual to find the presence of another diamond crystal that violates the surface of the stone. Unfortunately, it is common for cutters and polishers to overlook this imperfection. Tiffany returns diamonds with knots to the marketplace.

Naturals

When faceting a diamond, a cutter may leave unpolished a part of the original crystal surface. This is called a "natural." Naturals may detract from the diamond's appearance. Tiffany gemologists reject unsightly naturals.

COLOR

LESS IS MORE

The term "color" may be misleading. This is because the ideal engagement diamond is characterized by a lack of color. That is to say, it is clear to the point of being colorless or nearly colorless.

The colored tinting found in most diamonds is caused by minute impurities within the stone. The untrained eye is incapable of making the accurate color evaluations that can affect the value of a stone by thousands of dollars.

At the Tiffany Gemological Laboratory, the color of each diamond is determined by measuring it against authenticated "master diamonds." Each stone is then color-graded to a precise scale from "D" (colorless) to "Z" (saturated).

Only diamonds "I" color or better are accepted by Tiffany.

Tiffany color grades all diamonds, regardless of any previous evaluations. Frequently Tiffany rejects stones and returns them to the marketplace. If a stone has a borderline color classification, Tiffany automatically gives it the lower grade.

It should be noted here that "fancy colored" diamonds may be highly valued and have their own separate grading standards.

Beware of Excessive Fluorescence
Certain diamonds exhibit a natural phenomenon that makes the stone glow when exposed to ultraviolet light. In certain store light this fluorescence can actually mask the color of a diamond, making it appear whiter than it really is. However, in natural light, intense fluorescence produces a diamond with a disappointing milky appearance. Tiffany will not accept diamonds that our Gemological Laboratory determines to have "strong" or "very strong" fluorescence.

CARAT WEIGHT

BEAUTY ON ANY SCALE

The weight of a diamond is measured in carats. One carat equals 0.20 grams. The Tiffany Gemological Laboratory measures diamonds to 1/1000th of a carat.

Carat weight alone does not determine a diamond's value. Two stones of equal weight can vary widely in price because of quality differences. In fact, a smaller diamond may actually be more beautiful than a larger stone with inferior cut, clarity, color, or presence.

When considering diamonds of equal quality, the larger stone will have considerably more value. Usually a 2-carat diamond will be more than twice as valuable as a 1-carat stone. Large diamonds of high quality are very rare.

The Tiffany Difference
On one key point, Tiffany's diamond standards are aesthetically and philosophically at odds with other jewelers. Every Tiffany diamond is cut to achieve the perfect balance of brilliance, dispersion, and scintillation. Others may choose to maximize carat weight through out-of-proportion table size or other tricks.

2.99

2.50

2.00

1.50

1.00

.75

.50

.25

.18

THE TIFFANY GEMOLOGICAL LABORATORY MEASURES DIAMONDS TO 1/1000TH OF A CARAT.

A TIFFANY DIAMOND IS AN EXEMPLAR OF PRECISION OF CUT, SYMMETRY, AND POLISH.

PRESENCE

AN EXCLUSIVE TIFFANY MEASURE OF INTEGRITY

Tiffany & Co. has additional and important diamond quality standards that reach well beyond the customary 4C's. These measures, which Tiffany collectively calls "presence," include precision of cut, symmetry, and polish. Individually, and as a group, they influence a diamond's brilliance, dispersion, scintillation, and overall appearance.

Precision of Cut
In any gem-quality diamond, but especially the Tiffany round-brilliant, the shape, size, and angle of each individual facet are crucially important. The expert diamond cutter must follow a prescribed geometric plan to produce an "excellent" precision of cut. And if the cutter has failed, the gemologists in the Tiffany Gemological Laboratory will quickly find the mistake and promptly reject the stone.

Symmetry
It sounds so simple, but it is not. The symmetry of a diamond is determined by a complex series of measurements and visual inspections. Each one contributes to the stone's rating. Tiffany demands a rating above the industry norm. Tiffany will not tolerate symmetry flaws such as significant:

Off-center tables
Off-center culets
Misshapen facets
Misaligned crowns and pavilions
Out-of-round girdle outlines
Wavy girdles
Non-parallel tables and girdles

NOTE SCRATCH IN UPPER HALF AND
POLISH LINES BELOW FACET JUNCTURE

CLOCKWISE FROM TOP RIGHT:
THE TIFFANY SETTING, LUCIDA AND
ETOILE ENGAGEMENT RINGS.

THE LUCIDA SETTING IS BOTH GRACEFUL
AND TIMELESS.

Polish

The quality of a diamond's polish is an oft-forgotten measure. And yet it clearly plays a key role in determining brilliance, dispersion, and scintillation. Tiffany demands a polish rating well above the industry norm. Tiffany will not tolerate polish flaws, such as significant:

Abrasions

Subadamantine luster

Nicks, pits, scratches

Polish lines and marks

TIFFANY STANDARDS FOR
THE SETTING

IMPORTANT AND BEAUTIFUL DETAIL

EVERY TIFFANY SETTING
IS CUSTOMIZED TO
ACCOMMODATE THE SPECIFIC SIZE
AND SHAPE OF THE DIAMOND.
THIS ATTENTION TO PROPORTION,
INDIVIDUAL SCALE, AND
HAND CRAFTSMANSHIP IS UNIQUE
IN THE JEWELRY BUSINESS.

DESIGN

CRAFTSMANSHIP

METALLURGY

DESIGN

It has often been noted that great design follows function. There are no finer examples of this axiom than the diamond ring settings of Tiffany.

In a Tiffany diamond ring there can be only one star—the diamond.

Customized

Every Tiffany setting is customized to the stone. The Tiffany setting is individually designed to respectfully embrace the size and shape of the diamond. The stone is always held by the girdle so as not to block the light entering and exiting the diamond. The prongs are thick enough to securely hold the stone yet thin enough to be graceful and beautiful.

Each ring is thoughtfully designed to be perfectly balanced with tempered proportions and to be always aesthetically and geometrically pleasing. Design gimmicks and fads look foolish over time and are, therefore, assiduously avoided.

It has been estimated that over her lifetime a woman looks at her engagement ring one million times. A Tiffany ring ensures that this experience is always rewarding.

NOTE HOW THE CAREFULLY TAPERED PRONGS IN THE TIFFANY SETTING "HUG" THE GIRDLE WITHOUT VIOLATING THE TABLE.

INSIDE EVERY RING, TIFFANY PROUDLY ENGRAVES ITS NAME AND THE FINENESS OF THE METAL.

THE ENGAGEMENT RINGS OF TIFFANY.

CRAFTSMANSHIP

A Tiffany diamond ring is created by Tiffany jewelers who have unparalleled skill, patience, and discipline. Each aspect of the ring, including the inside of the mounting, is hand finished and hand polished.

Strong Prongs

It is the duty of every Tiffany setting to protect the diamond from loss or damage. In the crafting of a diamond ring, the positioning of the prongs around the diamond is a delicate task requiring great skill. Inferior prong adjustment is unacceptable. Damaging a diamond because of indelicate craftsmanship is inexcusable.

Inspections

At every step in the crafting process the ring is fully inspected. Special attention is focused on the mounting and shank assembly and the stone setting. The final inspection process assures that the metal has a beautiful, satin-smooth finish, free of significant scratches.

METALLURGY

A lifetime purchase produces requirements well beyond the norm. Such is the mandate of a Tiffany ring. Tiffany metals, whether platinum or gold, have the utmost integrity in all standards.

Tiffany Platinum

Platinum is the ideal choice for showcasing diamonds. Aesthetically, its neutral coloring maximizes the diamond's white light. However, it is the durability and hardness of this precious metal that is especially important.

Tiffany platinum is notable for its perfection, .950 pure. In addition, from the moment the molten metal is cast, great care is taken to be sure it is free of air bubbles and foreign matter that can weaken or discolor the metal. After casting, a full inspection is made.

Tiffany Gold

Tiffany gold is beyond reproach as well: 18-karat yellow gold, .750 pure. Interestingly, Tiffany's gold engagement rings feature platinum prongs or bezels so as not to discolor the white light emanating from the stone.

THE DIAMOND RINGS OF TIFFANY

Every Tiffany diamond ring is celebrated for its superlative beauty. The various gemological standards for all the legendary Tiffany diamond shapes, while different, are just as rigorous as those for the round-brilliant shape discussed in these pages.

The Tiffany Setting

Around the world, the Tiffany Setting is the most honored and recognized engagement ring ever. Since its inception well over a century ago, this ring has been copied but never equaled. The ingenious six-prong setting lifts the diamond up into the light where its fine faceting can release its brilliance, dispersion, and scintillation.

Lucida

The Lucida Setting was designed with just one particular stone in mind: the Lucida Diamond. The powerful sweep of lines, like ancient flying buttresses, proudly presents the inimitable and patented step-cut and brilliant Lucida Diamond. This is pure Tiffany design. The rectangular Lucida Diamond has the same proud qualities as the square classic.

Etoile

Modern and streamlined, yet perfectly timeless, Etoile is a symphony of harmonious curves. It is interesting to note that every gold Etoile ring embraces the diamond in a platinum cradle so that the integrity of the white light is not compromised.

Three Stones
Tiffany three-stone diamond rings are distinguished by their remarkable beauty and attention to detail. No jeweler takes more care when matching side stones for cut, clarity, color, carat weight, and presence. Tiffany pays particular attention to the elevation and design balance between the side stones and center diamond.

Three Stones with Color
Rubies, sapphires, or emeralds, together with diamonds, create a stunning engagement ring. Tiffany takes great pride and care in finding the best of these precious stones and crafting a timeless design.

Fancy Shapes
Tiffany offers a remarkable selection of fancy-shaped diamond rings, some beautifully complemented with side stones. Historically, each of these shapes and special designs has had a devoted following.

Other Styles
Over the years the designers of Tiffany have created a myriad of extraordinary ring designs beyond the traditional classics. These may be chosen for an engagement ring or to celebrate a special occasion.

THE TIFFANY SETTING.

LUCIDA.

ETOILE.

THREE STONES.

THREE STONES WITH COLOR.

FANCY SHAPES FROM LEFT: PEAR, CUT-CORNER EMERALD, ROUND, OVAL, MARQUISE, AND TRADITIONAL EMERALD.

OTHER STYLES.

DIAMOND-BAND RINGS OF TIFFANY.

THE TIFFANY DIAMOND CERTIFICATE
PRESENTS PRECISE GRADING DATA ON
CUT, CLARITY, COLOR, CARAT WEIGHT,
AND PRESENCE.

DIAMOND-BAND RINGS

A wedding band should enhance the
beauty of an engagement ring. And, at
the same time, it must have the character
and design integrity to be worn alone.
Tiffany band ring designs succeed
triumphantly by both measures.

THE TIFFANY DIAMOND
CERTIFICATE

The Tiffany Diamond Certificate is
awarded by Tiffany & Co. This document
warrants the authenticity and integrity of
a Tiffany diamond. Unlike the documen-
tation that may accompany stones purchased elsewhere, the Tiffany Diamond
Certificate is an actual guarantee.

The Tiffany Diamond Certificate
provides reassurance for today and many
years from now.

THE TIFFANY PROMISE

THE WOMAN WHO RECEIVES A
TIFFANY RING WILL ALWAYS KNOW
THAT HER RING IS SUPERLATIVE.
IN THE YEARS TO COME,
TIFFANY & CO.
WILL ALWAYS BE THERE
TO STAND BEHIND THE PURCHASE.

INDEX

COLLECTIONS CREDITS

ACKNOWLEDGMENTS

The author and Tiffany & Co. would first like to thank Michael Kowalski, chairman and chief executive officer, for his confidence and his most generous and vital support.

We would like to give special recognition to: Eric Erickson, for contributing so much toward the illustrations of this book; Kay Olson Freeman, whose research into historical personages sheds much light on the story of *Tiffany Diamonds*; and Rollins Maxwell, whose historical research, picture research, and captions add richness and texture to the history of Tiffany's adventures in that wonderful world of diamonds. This book is as much theirs as it is the author's.

We are also grateful to MaryAnn Aurora for calmly maintaining order over all the complex materials and personalities that went into the creation of this book; Eric Himmel, editor in chief of Harry N. Abrams, Inc., for his support of both the concept of this book and its realization; Harriet Whelchel, managing editor of Harry N. Abrams; Andrea Danese, our editor, for her vision and enthusiasm; Barbara Burn, our co-editor; and Darilyn Lowe Carnes, our designer at Abrams, for the beauty of her compositions.

We are grateful for the exceptional help offered by David Kelley, manager of the Tiffany photo studio, as well as the following for their generous help with photography: David Behl, Adam Campanella, Billy Cunningham, Carlton Davis, Martin Friedman, Jason Gallicher, Phil Garfield, Elizabeth Heyert, Hiro, Ryszard Horowitz, Thomas Milewski, James Moore, Victor Skrebneski, and Walter Thomson. We are also thankful for the support of AnnaMarie Sandecki, director of Tiffany Archives, and Louisa Bann, manager of research services at Tiffany Archives.

The following were invaluable for providing illustrations and/or advice, and all deserve our profound gratitude for making this book possible: The Field Museum, Chicago; The Louvre Museum, Paris; The Metropolitan Museum of Art, New York; The Museum of the City of New York; The Museum of Natural History, Smithsonian Institution; The New-York Historical Society; The New York Public Library, Astor and Tilden Foundations; The Royal Collection, Her Majesty Queen Elizabeth II; Art Resource, New York; Bettman/Corbis; N. Bloom & Son, London; Bridgeman Art Library International; Christie's; Ralph Esmerian; Mr. and Mrs. Paul Hallingby Jr.; Andrew Hart, vice president diamond division, Tiffany & Co.; Fred Leighton Rare Collectable Jewels, New York; Pierce MacGuire of Tiffany's Schlumberger jewelry division; Caroline Naggiar, senior vice president of marketing, Tiffany & Co.; The Primavera Gallery, New York; James Robinson, Inc., New York; Stephen–Russell, New York; and Sotheby's.

PROJECT MANAGER: Andrea Danese
EDITOR: Barbara Burn
DESIGNER: Darilyn Lowe Carnes
PRODUCTION MANAGER: Maria Pia Gramaglia

Library of Congress Cataloging-in-Publication Data

Loring, John.
  Tiffany diamonds / by John Loring.
    p. cm.
  Includes bibliographical references and index.
  ISBN 13: 978–0–8109–5937–8 (hardcover : alk. paper)
  ISBN 10: 0–8109–5937–2
  1. Tiffany and Company. 2. Diamond jewelry–History. I. Title.

NK7398.T5L657 2005
739.27'09747'1—dc22
            2005017020

Printed and bound in Japan
10 9 8 7 6 5 4 3 2

harry n. abrams, inc.
a subsidiary of La Martinière Groupe
115 West 18th Street
New York, NY 10011
www.hnabooks.com

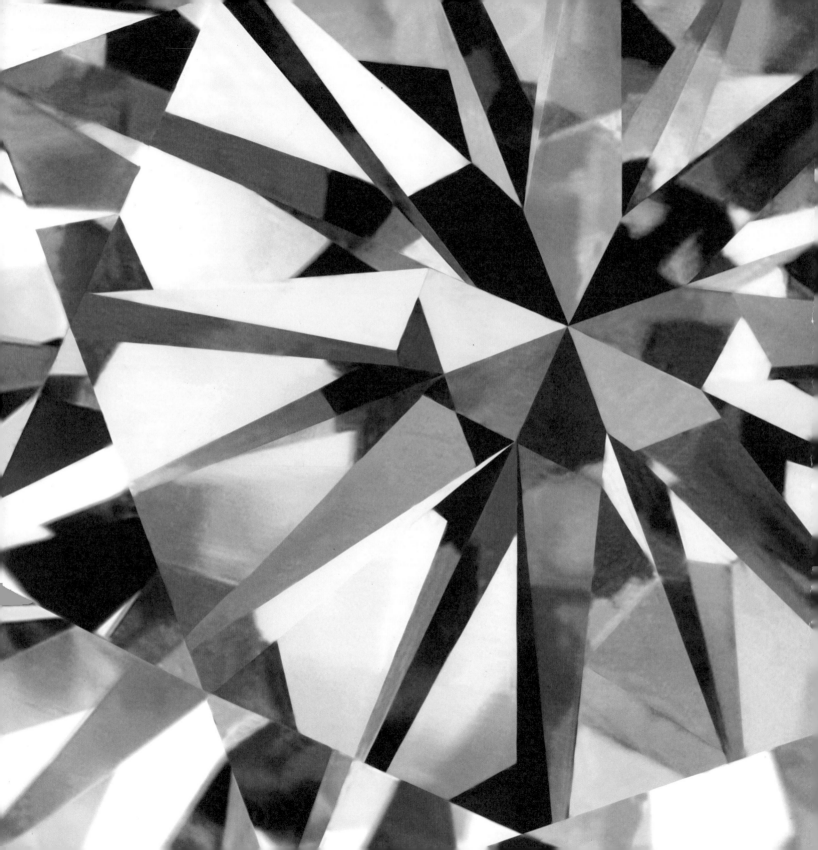